KETO RECIPES FOR WOMEN

The Top Secret Fast and Easy to Make Ketogenic Recipes for Women of All Ages – Live Healthier, Live Active, have a Flat Belly, and Reverse Common Diseases by Following a Perfect and Tested Ketogenic Diet Plan

KETO PREGNANCY COOKBOOK

KETO RECIPES FOR WOMEN OVER 50

KETO PREGNANCY COOKBOOK

Table of Contents

INTRODUCTION

The Keto diet (short for ketogenic diet) by and large requires devouring 75% of your everyday calories from fat, 20% from protein and only 5% from sugars. Dissimilar to some low-carb diets that suggests nixing sugar and prepared grains (like white bread and pasta); going on the Keto diet likewise implies disposing of practically all carbs from your diet, including natural products, entire grains and a few vegetables. Why? Carbs are the body's favored fuel source; when the body runs out of carbs to consume, it goes to fat and protein, a state called ketosis. This can prompt fast weight reduction.

Keto diet advocates say that eating this way expands energy brings down diabetes hazard and assists you with shedding pounds rapidly with no craving. However, the science behind Keto is exceptionally restricted, with not very many clinical examinations in people. Scientists have advised that there's still a great deal we don't think about how high-fat, low-carb eating impacts long haul wellbeing.

Is the Keto diet protected during pregnancy?

With regards to the Keto diet and pregnancy, research is considerably more difficult to find. There haven't been any controlled investigations done in pregnant human ladies as testing on this gathering is, naturally, debilitate. Notwithstanding, pregnant mice took care of a ketogenic diet experienced numerous issues with their posterity, including more slow development, more modest hearts and cerebrums and an enlarged spine. "A ketogenic diet during incubation is related with organ brokenness and possibly social changes in post pregnancy life," as indicated by the examination, distributed in BMC Pregnancy and Childbirth.

"The Keto diet is basically undependable for pregnant ladies showing the body to utilize ketones rather than glucose—doesn't work for developing children. "Glucose, from sugars, is the essential fuel hotspot for child's development and advancement and not having sufficient glucose can cause significant issues,"

Not exclusively can the Keto diet lead to formative postponements in your child yet it can likewise cause wholesome inadequacies whenever done erroneously, which can prompt major issues for both pregnant ladies and their children, says Lily Nichols, RDN, CDE, creator of Real Food for Pregnancy. Numerous individuals who follow the Keto diet carefully don't eat food sources like natural products, nuts, beans, and numerous vegetables—wellsprings of fundamental micronutrients important for the solid advancement of your infant.

This doesn't mean you ought to eat all the carbs constantly and in the event that you've learned in the past that your body reacts well to a lower-carb diet, it's fine to proceed with that, "I am one of only a handful few dietitians who stands up on the side of lower-carb diets during pregnancy, yet it doesn't need to be a win or bust circumstance; you can get the beneficial outcomes from decreasing your carbs without going full Keto,"

The key is to recall that not all sugars are made similarly. The two specialists suggest removing basic carbs from low quality nourishments like treats, sweet oats, candy, chips, pop and frozen yogurt yet keeping sound carbs like berries, apples, beans, yams and squash.

Keto meals for Pregnancy

40 recipes

1.   Spicy Red Pasta with Lentils

PREP TIME 5 minutes COOK TIME 25 minutes TOTAL TIME 30 minutes Servings: 2

INGREDIENTS:

- LENTILS
- 1/2 cup dry red lentils (washed in cool water for 1 moment)
- 2 cups water
- 1 squeeze ocean salt
- PASTA SAUCE
- 1 Tbsp. olive oil
- 3 cloves garlic, minced (3 cloves yield ~1 1/2 Tbsp.)
- 1/4 cup carrots (finely diced)
- 1/4 cup diced tomatoes (optional)
- 1 15-ounce can tomato sauce*
- 2 Tbsp. tomato paste

- 1 squeeze ocean salt (in addition to additional to taste)
- 1/2 tsp. red stew chips (isolated)
- 1 Tbsp. dried or new oregano
- 1 Tbsp. dried or new basil
- 1-2 Tbsp. sugar of decision, (for example, natural unadulterated sweetener or coconut sugar)
- 1 Tbsp. veggie lover parmesan cheddar (optional/in addition to additional to taste)
- FOR SERVING
- 8 ounces without gluten pasta (I like Trader Joe's Gluten Free Fussili, or sub carrot noodles)

DIRECTIONS:

1. Add lentils and water to a little pan and bring to a low bubble over medium heat, at that point lessen heat marginally to accomplish a gentle stew (not bubble).
2. Cook lentils to favored doneness - 15 minutes for a slight chomp, 20-22 minutes for more delicate lentils. For this dish, I lean toward 'still somewhat firm' so they don't get soft.
3. At the point when lentils are done cooking, channel off any overabundance cooking fluid, season with a spot of salt, and put in a safe spot.
4. While lentils are cooking, heat a large, rimmed metal or cast iron skillet over medium heat. When hot, add olive oil, garlic, carrots and tomato (optional). Sauté for 3 minutes, mixing regularly.
5. To forestall splattering, eliminate skillet from heat and add pureed tomatoes, tomato paste,

squeeze ocean salt, stew drop, oregano, basil, sugar, and vegetarian parmesan cheddar (optional), and mix to consolidate.

6. Spot back over heat and bring to a low stew over medium-low heat. When stewing, lessen heat to low and keep cooking for 10-15 minutes, mixing once in a while.

7. In the case of presenting with pasta, cook as per bundle DIRECTIONS right now. At that point channel and put in a safe spot.

8. Test pasta sauce and change flavors depending on the situation. Add more sugar to adjust and improve the flavors: bean stew chip for heat, salt for pungency, or more spices for profundity of flavor. On the off chance that excessively thick, meager with a little water.

9. Add the cooked, depleted lentils to the sauce and mix to join. To serve, either spoon sauce over noodles, or add pasta to the sauce and throw to cover.

10. Present with any extra fixings, for example, red pepper chips, vegetarian parmesan cheddar, and new basil.

11. Best when new. Store extras independently in the fridge as long as 3 days. Reheat sauce in the microwave or pan. Add a little water to thin if excessively thick. I've discovered gluten free pasta doesn't keep well, so cook new for each cluster.

12. Notes

13. *Tomato sauce is pureed tomatoes that are pre-prepared with flavors like garlic, salt, pepper, and oregano, and is unique in relation to plain puréed tomatoes. Change the sauce if

using squashed tomatoes or purée by adding more flavors to taste (for example garlic powder, dried or new basil and oregano, ocean salt and sugar of decision)

2. Keto BBQ Chickpea Pizza

Prep Time: 15 minutes Cook Time: 45 minutes Total Time: 1 hour Servings: 4 servings

INGREDIENTS:

- For the pizza outside layer:
- 2 1/4 teaspoons yeast
- 1 cup tepid water isolated
- A spot of sugar
- 2 1/2 cups bread flour isolated
- 2 tablespoons olive oil
- 1 teaspoon salt
- For the pizza garnishes:
- 2 tablespoons olive oil
- 1 large yellow onion meagerly cut
- Salt and dark pepper to taste
- 1 tablespoon water
- 1 red ringer pepper cultivated and meagerly cut
- 1 14.5-ounce can chickpeas, depleted, flushed, and dried
- 1/3 - 1/2 cup grill sauce
- 8 ounces gouda ground

DIRECTIONS:

1. For the outside layer, in a little bowl whisk together the yeast, 1/4 cup of water, and a touch of sugar. Allow the blend to sit while you set up the remainder of the mixture. In the interim, in the bowl of a stand blender fitted with the bread snare connection, join 2 cups of bread flour, olive oil, salt, and remaining water. At the point when the yeast gets frothy, add it into the bowl with the flour. (In the event that the yeast doesn't get frothy, it very well might be dead and you'll need to begin once again with new yeast.)

2. Blend the batter on medium speed until very much consolidated. In the event that the batter is as yet adhering to the sides of the bowl following a moment or blending, at that point include more flour. Blend on medium-fast for 4 minutes. Cover gently with saran wrap and let the batter ascend in a warm, without draft place until multiplied in size, around 30 minutes.

3. In the mean time, heat the oven to 425ºF.

4. In a large skillet, heat the leftover olive oil over medium heat. Add the onions to the container alongside a sprinkle of salt. Sauté for 8-10 minutes, blending like clockwork, until beginning to caramelize and brown. Add a tablespoon of water to the container and sauté for another 3-4 minutes. Mix in the ringer pepper cuts and sauté until delicate and beginning to brown, around 3-4 minutes. Mix in the chickpeas. Season to taste with salt and dark pepper.

5. Oil a 12-inch oven-verification dish or cast-iron skillet. Spread the mixture in the skillet with the goal that it arrives along the edges. Top with 1/3 cup of the grill sauce, spreading it around the batter and leaving a 1/2-inch edge for the covering. Top with the ground cheddar and the vegetable chickpea combination. Sprinkle with 1-2 tablespoons of extra grill sauce, or to taste.
6. Put the container in the oven and prepare for 15 minutes or until the cheddar is gurgling and the lower part of the batter is brilliant brown. Let cool for 5 minutes.

3. Low-carb, baked kale, and broccoli salad

Time 10 + 20 + 3 minutes | Servings 2

INGREDIENTS:
- Broccoli florets
- Bare minced meat

DIRECTIONS:
1. Set aside.
2. (2.5 cm) higher than
3. The eggs. Cover and bring to a boil over high heat. Cook once, remove from
4. heat and boil in water, depending on preference: 10-12 minutes (hard-
5. Cooked), or 6-8 minutes (medium cooked), or 5-6 minutes (soft boiled).
6. Meanwhile, set aside a bowl of ice-cold water.
7. To peel. Peel under running water and cut into halves or quarters. Set
8. Aside.
9. Add the sliced garlic and fry until golden brown. Remove the garlic from the pan and place it on kitchen paper too crispy. Keep the garlic-infused oil in the pan.
10. With the olive oil. Add the broccoli, kale, and spring onions. Use pliers, throw to

11. Coat and bake for about 5 minutes, or until lightly cooked.
12. Board with the eggs, avocado, and mustard mayonnaise.

4. Low-carb asparagus salad with walnuts

INGREDIENTS:
- Fresh mint, for decoration

DIRECTIONS:
1. Minutes, or until light golden brown
2. the bottom ends, which are quite stringy and chewy
3. Then cut the remaining asparagus into thin, sloping asparagus slices.
4. Add the hot chili flakes, salt, and avocado
5. Oil and olive oil.
6. Mix the beat gently but well with a rubber spatula.

5. Keto Apricot Corn Muffins

YIELD: It makes six large muffins. |MIXING TIME: 10 minutes |BAKING: 375°F for about 20 minutes

INGREDIENTS:

- 1 cup fine-grind stoneground yellow cornmeal
- 1 cup unbleached all-purpose flour
- 1 tsp. baking powder
- 1 tsp. Baking soda
- ½ tsp. kosher salt
- ½ cup whole milk
- 6 tbsp. unsalted butter, melted
- 13 cup pure maple syrup
- Two large eggs
- ½ cup dried apricots, coarsely chopped.

6. Keto low carb Lemon Garlic Chicken

Total Time Prep: 20 min. + marinating Bake: 40 min. Makes 6 servings

INGREDIENTS:

- 1/4 cup olive oil
- 2 tablespoons lemon juice
- 3 garlic cloves, minced
- 1-1/2 teaspoons minced new thyme or 3/4 teaspoon dried thyme
- 1 teaspoon salt
- 1/2 teaspoon minced new rosemary or 1/4 teaspoon dried rosemary, squashed
- 1/4 teaspoon pepper
- 6 bone-in chicken thighs
- 6 chicken drumsticks
- 1 pound child red potatoes, split
- 1 medium lemon, cut
- 2 tablespoons minced new parsley

DIRECTIONS:

1. Preheat oven to 425°. In a little bowl, whisk the initial 7 INGREDIENTS until mixed. Pour 1/4 cup marinade into an enormous bowl or shallow dish. Add chicken and go to cover. Refrigerate 30 minutes. Cover and refrigerate remaining marinade.

2. Channel chicken, disposing of any leftover marinade in bowl. Spot chicken in a 15x10x1-in. heating container; add potatoes in a solitary layer. Shower held marinade over potatoes; top with lemon cuts. Prepare until a thermometer embedded in chicken peruses 170°-175° and potatoes are delicate, 40-45 minutes. Whenever wanted, cook chicken 3-4 crawls from heat until profound brilliant brown, around 3-4 minutes. Sprinkle with parsley prior to serving.

7. Keto Pizza Hut Cavatina

INGREDIENTS:
- 1-green pepper chopped
- 1/4 pound Shell noodles
- Cut 1-onion into thin slices
- 1/4 pound of pasta
- 8-ounces of grated mozzarella
- 1/2 pound hamburger brown
- 8 grams of grated Parmesan cheese
- 1/2 pound Italian sausage brown

DIRECTIONS:
1. Cook noodles in the course of the package. Heat the sauce and mix it with the hamburger and the fried sausage. Sprinkled with Pam cooking spray, noodles, and sauce layers in 11 X 13 pans. Layer pepperoni, green peppers, and onions, mushrooms, and cheese. Make about 3-layers of cheese and cover with it. Baking
2. For about forty-five minutes in 350 stages or until the cheese is melted.

8. Keto Spaghetti Pizza Recipe

INGREDIENTS:
- 500 g ground beef
- 500 g of spaghetti
- 400 g tomatoes cut into small cubes
- 150 g sliced pepperoni
- 1 ½ cups of shredded cheddar cheese
- 1-cup of grated Swiss cheese
- ½ cup of grated Parmesan cheese
- ½ cup of whole milk
- 1-chopped onion
- 3-cloves of garlic, finely chopped
- 2-finely chopped red or green peppers

DIRECTIONS:
1. Gather them to make the spaghetti pizza.
2. Preheat the oven to 170 ° C. Boil a large pot of water to cook the spaghetti.
3. Cook the beef, chopped onion, chopped garlic, and chopped red and inexperienced peppers in a saucepan over medium heat with oil until the meat is browned.

4. Drain well, upload the pasta sauce, cut the tomatoes into small cubes, and the Italian seasoning. Stir well and cook over medium heat while you prepare the spaghetti.
5. Cook the statements under the bundle instructions.
6. Combine the milk, eggs, and grated Parmesan cheese in a large bowl and beat until blended.
7. Strain the spaghetti and stir with the egg aggregate. Spread half of the spaghetti, egg, and milk mixture in an ovenproof dish and copper with half of the sauce and red meat combination. Repeat the layers. Bake in a preheated oven for 30 or 40 minutes until hot and cover with the closing cheeses, then the pepperoni. Return to the new and bake until the cheeses melt. Let stand for 5 minutes and cut into squares to serve the spaghetti pizza.

9. Keto Garden Spaghetti

INGREDIENTS:
- 1 liter of milk
- 1/8 teaspoon of pepper
- 1/2 teaspoon of salt
- 18 oz. bacon sliced extra thick
- 1/4 cup of olive oil
- 12 oz. sliced mushrooms
- 6-tablespoons of chopped shallots
- Cook 1-pound of spaghetti according to the package insert
- 2-teaspoons finely chopped parsley

DIRECTIONS:
1. Melt butter over medium heat in a 4-quart casserole.
2. Remove the meal and prepare dinner for 1 minute. Add milk, pepper, and pepper, and start with a wire beater until the mixture boils slightly. Reduce the heat and cook for 5 minutes, even if the sauce thickens. Stir the Fontina cheese into the sauce and let it soften in the sauce. Stay warm.

3. Prepare the bacon thoroughly for dinner. Drain on paper towels. Cut into 1/4-inch pieces and whisk in the sauce. In a large skillet, soften the olive oil over medium heat. Attach sliced onions and chopped mushrooms and fry until golden brown; adhere to the sauce. Cook spaghetti in the direction of the box. Drain well and add the parsley to the sauce. Mix well and move to a serving table. Sprinkle with Parmesan cheese and let it function as quickly as possible.

10. Keto Spaghetti Frittata

INGREDIENTS:
- 2-tablespoons of olive oil
- 1-tablespoon of butter
- ¼ cup of milk
- 2 cups of grated Parmesan cheese
- ½ teaspoon of dried basil leaves
- 1-cup cooked spaghetti or fettuccine cut into 5cm pieces

DIRECTION:
1. Heat the olive oil and butter in a pan until it melts.
2. Add the green pepper and cook the dinner over medium heat, frequently stirring until soft and crispy.
3. Meanwhile, in a large bowl, combine the eggs with the milk, ¼ cup of grated Parmesan cheese, salt and pepper, and basil.
4. Add the cooked pasta to the egg combination and stir gently.
5. Then upload the egg combination to the pan and spread the Pasta in a uniform layer.

6. Cook the egg combination over medium heat, occasionally raising the edges with a spatula so that the uncooked egg flows underneath.
7. When the egg aggregate is almost done but still moist, cover with grated Parmesan cheese after 10 minutes. Cook for a few more minutes until it starts to brown. Remove from oven and cut the spaghetti frittata into portions. Serve immediately.

11. Keto Savory Oat Porridge With Greens And Egg

Prep Time: 5 minutes | Cook Time: 10 minutes | Total Time: 15 minutes | Servings: 1 serve

INGREDIENTS:
- 1/2 cup moved oats
- 1/2 medium zucchini
- 1 modest bunch child spinach
- 1/2 cup unsweetened almond milk
- 1/4 tsp. salt
- 1 tbsp. wholesome yeast chips
- 1 egg
- Optional
- 1 tbsp. pumpkin seeds as a garnish
- 1-2 tbsp. unflavored protein powder on the off chance that you need to add more protein to the morning meal

DIRECTIONS:

1. Mesh the zucchini (or hack into exceptionally meager matchsticks or minuscule dice, in the event that you can't be messed with the grater).
2. Pop the ground zucchini into a little pot along with the oats and almond milk, in addition to a large portion of some water. On the oven, bring to bubble and afterward diminish the heat. Cook, mixing periodically, for 7 to 10 minutes, until delicate and velvety; add some additional water or milk as you go on the off chance that you need to thin it out further. *If you are using protein powder also mix this in while the oats are cooking.
3. During the cooking, sprinkle in the salt and dietary yeast; trial and add additional flavoring whenever desired. Towards the last moment of the cooking, include the modest bunch of spinach so it shrivels into the oats.
4. Poach or fry the egg as you like to finish your bowl off with.
5. Serve the warm oats in a bowl with the poached egg. In the case of using them, add the pumpkin seeds on top for crunch.
6. Notes
7. I like to add a tablespoon or two of unflavored protein powder to my oats bowl to help the protein substance and make this a really fulfilling feast. This is completely optional and the oats bowl is similarly as yummy without it, obviously!

8. I suggest using almond milk in this formula since it has an unbiased, nutty flavor that loans itself well to an exquisite dish. Rice and additionally coconut milks are normally better so they probably won't function too. On the off chance that you endure dairy, cows or goats milk would function admirably in this formula too!

12. Keto Healthy Peach Cobbler

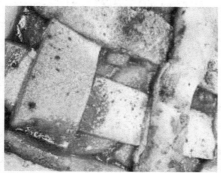

Prep Time15 minutes Cook Time1 hour 15 minutes refrigerate crust30 minutes Total Time2 hours Servings6 Calories547kcal

INGREDIENTS:

- Covering
- 4 cups whitened almond flour
- 1/2 teaspoon salt
- 1/2 cup sugar or sugar
- 2 eggs
- 6 tablespoons unsalted margarine softened
- Peach Filling
- 1/2 cup unsalted margarine 1 stick
- 1/2 cup brown sugar or light brown sugar
- 1/2 cup sugar or sugar
- 1 teaspoon cinnamon
- 1/2 teaspoon nutmeg
- 1/2 new lemon, juice of about 2-3 tablespoons.
- 2 teaspoons vanilla pure concentrate, not impersonation.

- 20 oz. frozen peaches this is typically 1 enormous pack. Or then again you can join various. See notes for canned or new peaches.
- 1 teaspoon cornstarch for sans gluten, use without gluten flour.
- 1 teaspoon water
- 1 egg Beaten with 1 teaspoon of water for egg wash
- cinnamon for fixing

DIRECTIONS:
1. Outside
2. Add the almond flour, sugar, and salt (dry INGREDIENTS to a blending bowl. Mix to consolidate.
3. Add the eggs and dissolved spread (wet INGREDIENTS to a different bowl and mix.
4. Add the dry INGREDIENTS to a food processor. Then, pour in the wet INGREDIENTS physically beat until the blend is fused. You can likewise consolidate the dry and wet INGREDIENTS in a blending bowl and blend by hand, however subsequent to testing; the best outcomes are using a food processor.
5. Eliminate the mixture and fold it up into an enormous ball. Cut the batter fifty-fifty. One half will be utilized for the base outside of the shoemaker.
6. Sprinkle a level surface with a little almond flour to keep the batter from staying. Utilize a carrying pin and carry out the mixture until level.
7. Refrigerate the batter for 30 minutes to expedite prior to dealing with. It will be truly

tacky in the event that you skirt this progression. The more you refrigerate, the simpler it is to deal with. I refrigerate half of the batter after it has been carried out, my inclination. You can keep it in a ball on the off chance that you wish.

8. After you have refrigerated, cut portion of the batter into strips around 1 inch thick.
9. Filling
10. Preheat oven to 350 degrees.
11. Heat a pot or pot on medium heat and add the spread. At the point when liquefied, include the sugars, nutmeg, and cinnamon. Mix constantly. Permit the combination to cook until the sugar or sugar has softened.
12. Include the lemon juice and vanilla and mix. Pour in the peaches. Mix and permit the combination to cook for around 4-5 minutes to mollify the peaches.
13. Consolidate the cornstarch and water in a little bowl to make slurry. Mix it together and add it to the pot. Mix to completely consolidate. Permit the blend to cook for 10-12 minutes until the filling thickens and eliminate it from heat.
14. Amass and Bake
15. Splash a 8×8 preparing dish or a 9.5 inch pie skillet with cooking shower or oil.
16. Spot 1/2 of the pie outside layer into the lower part of a 8×8 heating dish.
17. Using an opened spoon, top the outside with the peaches combination. You need to utilize an opened spoon here with the goal that you don't add an excess of fluid to the shoemaker.

On the off chance that you utilize an excessive amount of fluid it will be runny. I add it using an opened spoon, and afterward I finish it off with one huge spoonful of fluid from the pot.

18. Add cuts of pie covering to the top. You can organize the outside anyway you wish. In the event that you have lopsided strips, you can shape two together to frame one. Remove the rest of any strips that are excessively long. Brush the covering with the egg wash and sprinkle with cinnamon.

19. Heat for 25 minutes. Now the covering will start to brown. Open the oven and tent the dish with foil. Don't completely cover, freely tent (it shouldn't contact the shoemaker). This will keep the shoemaker from browning a lot on the top as the inside keeps on heating.

20. Prepare for an extra 20-25 minutes. You can eliminate the foil following 15 minutes if the covering needs seriously browning.

21. Important notes for recipe: You can join the pie hull INGREDIENTS by hand. It will take somewhat more and can be hard to join the INGREDIENTS to deliver a smooth covering. I discover this way works best.

22. You can substitute brown sugar or sugar for white and utilize possibly white sugar in the event that you wish.

23. Loads of individuals make peach shoemaker with a top outside layer as it were. I'm a gigantic aficionado of the outside so I do both a base and top layer. You can slice the hull formula down the middle and do 1 layer in the event that you wish. In the event that you

lessen the measure of covering utilized in this formula (and utilize 1/2 as the top layer in particular) it will bring about the accompanying macros per serving: 251 calories, 20 grams fat, 9 grams of net carbs, and 7 grams of protein.

24. Or then again you can get serious about the top layer of the outside. This will make it simpler to make a thick cross section design in the event that you are searching for that.

25. While setting the covering into the lower part of the preparing dish, I like to utilize the lower part of a glass mug to straighten it out.

26. In the event that using canned peaches I suggest 20-24oz. At times you can just discover canned in 15.5oz servings. For this situation you may select to utilize a can and a half or go with fewer peaches. In the case of using canned, channel 1/2 of the fluid from the can prior to adding it to the pot. In the event that you utilize the entirety of the fluid the filling will turn out to be excessively soupy.

27. In the case of using new peaches, you should strip the peaches first. You may likewise need to adapt to taste. New peaches are frequently tarter and less sweet. Taste your filling over and again and add more sugar if vital.

28. In the event that you utilize locally acquired pie outside and customary sugar, the macros per serving are as per the following: 889 calories, 61 grams fat, 62 grams of net carbs, and 16 grams of protein.

29. There's an enormous contrast in insight regarding vanilla concentrate versus impersonation. Vanilla will taste much better.
30. On the off chance that you utilize locally acquired pie outside layer, the heat time will be reliable. You presumably will not have to tent the skillet with foil. Utilize your judgment. In the event that the outside begins to become a brilliant shade of brown inside 30 minutes, tent it.
31. This formula incorporates margarine. You can choose if the utilization of spread is sound or not for you. You can take a stab at using oils like coconut or avocado oil in the event that you wish.

13. Keto Fruits and Veggies for women

Preparation Time: 10 mins |Cooking Time: 25 mins |Total Time: 35 mins

INGREDIENTS:
- 1 Cauliflower
- 1 bell pepper
- 1 cup mushroom slices, fresh
- 1 cup asparagus, chopped
- 1 tbsp. Olive oil

DIRECTIONS:
1. Preheat the oven to 400 ° F (205 ° C). Cover a baking tray with a silicone mat (or foil or baking paper).
2. Cut your cauliflower and bell pepper into equal sized pieces.
3. Slice your mushrooms and chop your asparagus.
4. Drizzle all your vegetables with olive oil.
5. Spread cauliflower, bell pepper, and mushrooms on baking tray. Don't crowd them and leave room for asparagus.

6. Bake for 10 minutes.
7. Stir / turn the vegetables and add asparagus to the pan.
8. Bake for 15 minutes, stir / turn again (after about 7 minutes).
9. Comments
10. The roasting times of vegetables are not 100% reliable. The larger the pieces, the longer it takes to cook.
11. If you want crispier roasted vegetables, shorten the roasting time by a few minutes. If you want softer roasted vegetables, increase the roasting time by up to 10 minutes (except asparagus, which should increase by up to 5 minutes).

14. Chicken Meatballs and Cauliflower Rice with Coconut Herb Sauce

PREP: 25 MIN | COOKING: 20 MIN | TOTAL: 45 MIN | Servings 4

INGREDIENTS:
- MEATBALLS
- Non-stick spray
- 1-tablespoon of extra virgin olive oil
- ½ red onion
- 2-cloves of garlic, chopped
- 1 pound of ground chicken
- ¼ cup of chopped fresh parsley
- 1-tablespoon of Dijon mustard
- ¾ teaspoon of kosher salt
- ½ teaspoon of freshly ground black pepper
- SAUCE
- A 14-ounce of coconut milk
- 1¼ cups of chopped fresh parsley, divided
- 4-spring onions, roughly chopped
- 1-clove of garlic, peeled and crushed
- Peel and juice one lemon
- Kosher salt and freshly ground black pepper

- Red pepper flakes, to serve
- One recipe Cauliflower rice

DIRECTIONS:

1. MAKE THE MEATBALLS: Preheat oven to 375 ° F. Line a baking tray with aluminum foil and spray with nonstick cooking spray.
2. In a medium skillet, heat the olive oil over medium heat. Add the onion and sauté until tender, about 5 minutes. Add the garlic and sauté until fragrant, about 1 minute.
3. Transfer the onion and garlic to a medium bowl and allow cooling slightly. Stir in chicken, parsley, and mustard; Season with salt and pepper. Shape the mixture into two tablespoons large balls and place on the baking tray.
4. Fry the meatballs until firm and cooked for 17 to 20 minutes.
5. MAKE THE SAUCE: In the bowl of a food processor, combine the coconut milk, parsley, spring onions, garlic, lemon zest, and lemon juice and mix until smooth; Season with salt and pepper.
6. Sprinkle the meatballs with the red pepper flakes and the rest of the parsley. Serve over the cauliflower rice with the sauce.

15. Napa Cabbage Soup with chicken Meatballs and seafood shrimps

Prep time: 5 min Cook time: 25 min Serving 2-4

INGREDIENTS:

- Soup base
- 2 large slices ginger
- 3 to 4 green onions , chopped
- (Option 1) Quick pork and chicken broth
- 1/4 cup chopped pancetta (or bacon)
- 1 cup chicken stock (or 2 cups, if you want the soup to be extra rich) (Optional)
- (Option 2) Clear seafood broth
- 1/4 cup dried shrimp
- 1/4 cup dried scallops
- (Option 3) Easy broth
- 3 cups chicken stock (or pork stock)
- Meatballs
- 1/2 pound (230 grams) ground turkey (or ground pork)
- 1/4 cup finely chopped green onion (green part) (Optional)

- 1 tablespoon Shaoxing wine (or dry sherry or Japanese sake)
- 2 teaspoons or tamari for gluten-free
- 2 teaspoons potato starch
- 1 teaspoon ginger , grated
- 1 large egg
- 1/4 teaspoon salt
- 1 teaspoon sesame oil (or peanut oil, or vegetable oil)
- Soup base
- 2 enormous cuts ginger
- 3 to 4 green onions , chopped
- (Alternative 1) Quick pork and chicken stock
- 1/4 cup chopped pancetta (or bacon)
- 1 cup chicken stock (or 2 cups, in the event that you need the soup to be additional rich) (Optional)
- (Alternative 2) Clear fish stock
- 1/4 cup dried shrimp
- 1/4 cup dried scallops
- (Alternative 3) Easy stock
- 3 cups chicken stock (or pork stock)
- Meatballs
- 1/2 pound (230 grams) ground turkey (or ground pork)
- 1/4 cup finely chopped green onion (green part) (Optional)
- 1 tablespoon Shaoxing wine (or dry sherry or Japanese purpose)
- 2 teaspoons or tamari for sans gluten
- 2 teaspoons potato starch
- 1 teaspoon ginger , ground
- 1 huge egg
- 1/4 teaspoon salt

- 1 teaspoon sesame oil (or nut oil, or vegetable oil)
- Soup
- 6 to 8 huge Napa cabbage leaves , chopped (create 6 to 8 cups)
- 1/2 daikon radish, stripped and chopped (creates 2 cups) (Optional)
- 1 clump enoki mushrooms brilliant needle mushrooms, intense closures eliminated and isolated
- 1/2 (400g/14-ounces) block delicate tofu , chopped
- Ocean salt to taste

DIRECTIONS:

1. Soup base alternative 1 - Quick pork and chicken stock
2. Heat a 3.8-liter (4-quart) pot over medium heat and add the greasy pieces of the pancetta. At the point when it begins to sizzle, go to medium low heat. Blending once in a while, cook until the fat renders and the pancetta becomes brilliant.
3. Add the lean pieces of the pancetta. Keep cooking and blending until brown.
4. Add chicken stock and promptly utilize a spatula to scratch the brown pieces off the lower part of the pot. Add 2 cups water (add 1 cup water, if using 2 cups chicken stock; or 3 cups water + 1 tablespoon shellfish sauce or hoisin sauce, in the event that you would prefer not to utilize chicken stock), ginger, and green onion. Cook over high heat until

bubbling. Go to medium low heat. Cover and bubble for 5 minutes.

5. Soup base choice 2 - Clear fish stock
6. Flush dried scallops. Spot scallops in a little bowl and add water to cover. Rehydrate for 2 to 3 hours. Channel and attack little pieces.
7. Wash dried shrimp, move to a little bowl, and add water to cover. Rehydrate for 30 minutes. Channel and put in a safe spot.
8. Join the rehydrated scallops and shrimp, ginger, green onion, and 3 cups water in a 3.8-liter (4-quart) pot. Heat over high heat until bubbling. Go to medium heat. Cover and let stew for 5 minutes.
9. Soup base alternative 3 - Easy stock
10. Join chicken stock (or pork stock), ginger, and green onion in a 3.8-liter (4-quart) pot. Heat over high heat until bubbling. Go to medium heat. Cover and bubble for 5 minutes.
11. Meatballs
12. Consolidate every one of the INGREDIENTS for the meatballs in an enormous bowl. Mix until all INGREDIENTS are simply joined and structure a somewhat runny blend. Don't over-mix it. Let sit for 5 to 10 minutes.
13. Soup
14. Wash and cut veggies while letting the stock stew.
15. Add daikon radish into the soup pot. Cover and cook for 5 minutes.
16. Add the thick pieces of the Napa cabbage. Cover and cook for 5 minutes.

17. Add the green pieces of the Napa cabbage and enoki mushroom into the soup. Cook for 2 to 3 minutes.
18. You can change the flavoring now, by adding somewhat salt, if necessary.
19. Add delicate tofu. Push every one of the INGREDIENTS aside of the pot, to clear some space for the meatballs. (On the off chance that you need more space in the pot, you can take out a portion of the Napa cabbage leaves)
20. Utilize a spoon to scoop 1 to 1.5 tablespoons of the meatball blend and cautiously add it into the soup. Rehash this until you've made around 15 meatballs.
21. Cover the pot and stew until the meatballs are simply cooked through, 4 to 5 minutes. Mood killer heat promptly and eliminate the pot from the oven, keeping it covered.
22. Serve hot as a principle or side. To make it a full dinner, you can heat up certain noodles (or mung bean noodles or shirataki noodles) and add them into the soup toward the finish of cooking. For this situation, you should add a smidgen more salt or light soy sauce, to make the stock somewhat saltier. Thusly, it will taste perfectly with the noodles.

16. Keto Eggrolls

INGREDIENTS:
- 2-possibilities are very vegetables oil
- 1-chicken skinless, boneless, half cut
- 2-tablespoons finely chopped green onion
- 2-tablespoons min. Red bell pepper
- ⅓ cup of corn buns
- ¼ cup black beans, fried and drained
- 2-tablespoons from chopped spinach, thawed and drained
- 2-common things you can see
- ½ tablespoon ground beef for parsley
- ½ teaspoon ground cumin
- ½ teaspoon of chilli powder

DIRECTIONS:
1. Rub 1-tablespoon of vegetable oil over the chicken bread. In an interval of medium heat, cook the bird in step with the side for about 5 minutes, until the flesh is now not pink and the juices are clear. Remove from heat and set aside.
2. Heat the last 1-tablespoon of vegetable oil in a medium saucepan over medium heat. Stir in the green onion and purple pepper. Cook and stir for 5 minutes, until tender.

3. Choose a color and mix in one plan and the other. Mix in some, black is, spinach, jalapeno peppers, parsley, cumin, chili powder, salt, and cayenne pepper. Boil and stir for five minutes, and it will usually be mixed and soft. Leave it and stir More Jack chese cheat in or that it is more.

17. Keto Chipotle Guacamole

INGREDIENTS:

- 2-large Hass avocados halved and pitted
- 1-teaspoon of fresh lemon juice
- 1-teaspoon of fresh lime juice
- 1/4 cup red onion finely chopped
- 1/2 jalapeño chili stemmed, seeded, and finely chopped (see notes)
- 2-tablespoons cilantro leaves finely chopped
- salt
- Tortilla chips to serve

DIRECTIONS:

1. In a medium bowl, combine all INGREDIENTS juice, and lime juice. Puree until smooth. Stir in onion, cilantro, and jalapeños - season with salt. Serve with chips.
2. To cool, press an area in a bowl and plastic wrap directly onto the entire bottom of the guacamole to expose no element to air.

18. Italian Egg Bake

Preparation time 10 minutes | Cooking time 18 minutes | Total time 28 minutes | Yield 4.5 servings

INGREDIENTS:
- 4 ounces of diced pancetta
- 1/2 cup of chopped red onion (about 140 grams)
- 1/2 cup of chopped fresh oregano
- 1/2 cup of chopped fresh basil
- 1/4 cup of unsweetened almond milk
- 2/3 cup grated Parmesan cheese (extra for topping)
- 1/2 teaspoon of chopped garlic
- 1/4 teaspoon sea salt and pepper each (or to taste)
- 1/2 cup chopped fresh tomato
- 1 cup of tomato sauce
- 5 large cage-free eggs
- Red pepper flakes for garnish
- Oregano for garnish

DIRECTIONS:

1. Preheat the oven to 425 degrees F.
2. Fry the pancetta and onion together in an 8 inch cast iron skillet (or oven safe pan) for 2 minutes or until fragrant.
3. Remove from heat.
4. Beat together the almond milk and parmesan cheese. Reserve extra cheese for the topping.
5. Stir in the garlic, tomato, sea salt / pepper, tomato sauce and herbs.
6. Pour the milk tomato mixture over the cast iron skillet (or ovenproof pan) with the onion and pancetta.
7. Using a spatula, make 5 small slits in the pan (evenly spaced) where you can place the eggs so that the yolk doesn't break. Break 5 eggs on top of each crack. If you find you have an egg with a runny yolk, just mix it through the pan, but then add another egg with a solid yolk. Or discard the runny yolk.
8. Add any extra cheese to the eggs and place the skillet in the oven for 15-18 minutes or until the egg whites are set (the yolk softens) and the corners are brown. Baking times vary depending on the oven and the type of skillet being used.
9. Garnish with Italian parsley and red pepper flakes. To enjoy

19. Keto Pesto Corkscrew

INGREDIENTS:
- 4-medium zucchini (about 2-pieces), trimmed
- An example of this has been described
- 2 cups have fresh, fresh
- ¼ cup of pine nuts, toasted
- ¼ ½ dug Parmesan cheese
- 1/4 plus 2-tablespoons extra-virgin olive oil, divided
- 2-tablespoons lemon juice
- 1-large clove garnish, sure
- ½ teaspoon ground pepper
- $ 1, as is known, but in 1-inch versions

DIRECTIONS:
1. Use a spiral vegetable cutter to cut zucchini lengthwise into long, thin pieces. Give up the rest, and things won't be that long there. Place the zucchini in a colander and this with a quarter of the repeat. Let it dry for 15 to 30 minutes, and then squeeze gently to eliminate any excess liquid.

2. Meanwhile, add basil, pine nuts, Parmesan cheese, 1/4 cup oil, lemon juice, garlic, pepper, and 1/4 teaspoon salt in a mini food processor. Process until almost smooth.
3. Heat 1 tablespoon oil in a huge skillet or medium-high heat. Add chicken in another layer; Use the last 1/4 teaspoon of salt. I understand it will take about 5 minutes. Take a large bowl and eat it in 3 tablespoons of the meal.
4. Add the last 1-tablespoon oil to the pan. Add the drained zucchini noodles, and it's just about 2 to 3 minutes.

20. Alaskan Cod with Mustard Cream Sauce

(Ready in about 10 minutes | Servings 4)

INGREDIENTS:

- One tablespoon coconut oil
- 4 Alaskan cod fillets
- Salt and black pepper, to taste
- Six leaves basil,
- One teaspoon yellow mustard
- One teaspoon paprika
- ¼ teaspoon bay leaf
- 3 tbsp. cream cheese
- One teaspoon lemon zest
- One tablespoon parsley,
- ½ mug Greek-style yogurt
- One garlic clove,

DIRECTIONS:

1. Heat coconut oil in a cooking pan. Sear the ready-to-cook fish for 2 to 3 minutes per side. Garnish with salt and black pepper.
2. Mix all components for the sauce until everything is well mixed. Top the fish fillets with the sauce and serve garnished with basil leaves. Enjoy your meal!

21. Chicken Tortilla Soup

INGREDIENTS:
- 1-chicken fillet; chopped into small pieces
- ½ cup sweet corn
- 1 cup onion, chopped
- 3-tablespoons fresh cilantro, chopped
- 1 cup chicken stock
- Avocado to taste
- 1-can diced peppers and tomatoes (8 grams)
- Colby jack cheese to taste
- 1-splash of lime juice in an individual bowl
- Tortilla chips to taste
- 1 cup of water

DIRECTIONS:
1. In a large, deep saucepan over medium heat, combine the chicken stock with water, onion, chili, and tomatoes, corn and cilantro; bring the mixture to a boil, stirring occasionally.
2. Add the chicken pieces; stir well, and reduce heat to low.
3. Cook for a few minutes until the chicken is cooked.
4. Add tortilla chips, followed by avocado and cheese to taste in serving dishes.

5. Add soup and a squeeze of lime to the bowls. Serve hot and enjoy.

22. Barrel Chicken And Dumplings

INGREDIENTS:
- 2-cups of flour
- 1/2 teaspoon of baking powder
- 1-pinch of salt
- 2-tablespoons of butter
- 1 cup of milk
- 2 liters of chicken stock
- 3 cups of cooked chicken

DIRECTIONS:
1. Place the flour, baking powder, and salt in a bowl. Cut the butter into the dry substances with a fork or pastry knife. Stay in the milk; mix with a bottle to the end of a ball.
2. Sprinkle a piece of the surface with flour. You will need a rolling pin and something to cut the dumplings with. I would like to request a pizza cutter. I also like to use a small spatula to lift the dumplings off the cutting surface.

3. Roll out the dough thinly with a heavily floured rolling pin. Dip your cutter in flour and cut the dumplings into squares about 2x2 inches each. It's okay for them now, not to be exact. Just look at it. Some can be bigger, some smaller, and some can be funny shaped.
4. Cook them for about 15 to 20 minutes or until they don't taste doughy.

23. Keto Beef Chili

INGREDIENTS:
- 1 (29-ounce)-can of tomato paste
- 1 (15-ounce) can be drained
- 1-can (15 ounce) pinto beans, drained
- 1-large onion, chopped (about 1 1/2 pieces)
- 1/2 cup of celery
- 1/4 cup diced green bell pepper
- 1/4 cup chili powder
- 1-teaspoon of cumin
- 1 1/2 teaspoons garlic powder
- 1-teaspoon of salt
- 1/2 teaspoon ground black pepper
- 1/2 teaspoon oregano

DIRECTIONS:
1. In an instant, the ground pork; drain.
2. Place the drained red meat and remaining components in 6 hours.
3. Cover the jar; simmer for 1 to 1 1/2 hours, stirring every 15 minutes.
4. In a skillet, the ground beef brown; drain. Layout the drained meat and the last pieces in a gradual change, then go down and prepare dinner for four hours.

24. Keto chilli bowl

INGREDIENTS:
- For Chile:
- 4-pounds ground chuck - ground for chili
- 1½ cups yellow onions, chopped
- 16 ounces tomato sauce
- 1-tablespoon cooking oil
- 3¼ plus 1 cup of water
- 1-tablespoon masa harina
- For Chili Spice Blend:
- 1-tablespoon paprika
- ½ cup of chili powder
- 1-teaspoon ground black pepper
- 1/8 cup of ground cumin

DIRECTIONS:
1. Mix the whole chili seasoning INGREDIENTS in a small bowl; still, mix until thoroughly mixed.
2. Now, in a 6-quart stockpot over medium heat; place and cook the meat until brown; drain. In the meantime, combine the chili spice mix in addition to the spaghetti sauce and 3¼ cups of water in the bowl; stir the INGREDIENTS well until well blended.

3. Add the chili spice liquid to the browned meat; stir well, and bring the mixture to a boil over medium heat.
4. In a large frying pan over medium heat; Heat 1 tablespoon of the vegetable oil and fry the onions for a few minutes until translucent. Add the fried onions to the chili.

25. Keto Chicken Enchilada Soup

INGREDIENTS:
- 2-rotisserie chickens or 3 pounds of cooked diced chicken
- ½ pound of processed American cheese; cut into small cubes
- 3-cups yellow onions, diced
- ¼ cup chicken crust
- 2-cups Masa Harina
- ½ teaspoon cayenne pepper
- 2-teaspoons garlic granules
- 1 - 2 teaspoons salt or to taste
- 2 cups tomatoes, crushed
- ½ cup vegetable oil
- 2-teaspoons chili powder
- 4 liters water
- 2-teaspoons ground cumin

DIRECTIONS:
1. In a large saucepan over medium heat, combine the oil with onions, chicken base, garlic granules, chili powder, cumin, cayenne, and salt. Cook for 3 to 5 minutes, until the onions are soft and translucent, stirring occasionally.

2. Mix 1 liter of water with masa Harina in a large cup or jug.
3. Keep stirring until there are no more lumps. Add the onions; bring the mixture to a boil over medium heat.
4. Once ready, cook for a few minutes, stirring constantly. Stir in tomatoes and the remaining 3 liters of water. Bring the soup to a boil again, stirring occasionally. Add the cheese.
5. Cook until cheese is completely melted, stirring occasionally. Add the chicken

26. Keto Thai Chicken Coconut Milk Soup

INGREDIENTS:
- 1-lemongrass stem
- 6-cups of chicken stock
- 2-chicken fillets
- 4-kaffir lime leaves
- 2-fresh and finely chopped red chilies
- 1-inch size piece and grated
- 400 ml of good quality coconut milk
- 2-tablespoons fish fumet (or more to taste)
- 2-tablespoons of lemon juice
- A handful of fresh basil leaves
- A handful of fresh cilantro leaves

DIRECTION:
1. Slice and chop the bottom of the lemongrass stalk. Save the top stem for later.
2. Place the chicken stock in a huge saucepan and produce to medium heat. If you have leftover chook or turkey bones, upload them too.
3. Then upload the lemongrass, top stem, kaffir lime leaves, and fresh chilies.
4. Cook for 5 to 8 minutes or until poultry is cooked through. Reduce the heat to medium.

5. Add ginger, two hundred ml coconut milk, fish sauce, and extra vegetables (if using). Stir well and let it simmer for a few minutes. Reduce the heat.
6. Add the lime juice and stir.
7. Make a taste test. Find the stability between sour, spicy, salty, and candy flavors. Start with salinity; if the soup is not salty or tasty enough add more fish fumet, a tablespoon at a time. If it's very bitter for miles, upload brown sugar.

27. Keto Corn Cream Recipe

INGREDIENTS:
- 1-ear of corn
- 1-yellow pepper
- 1-onion
- 1-tablespoon of butter
- 1-dash of cream
- Vegetable soup
- 1-dash of extra virgin olive oil

DIRECTION:
1. Put the butter in a pan and brown the previously peeled and finely chopped onion.
2. When the onion is transparent, add the yellow bell pepper cut into small cubes along with the corn and a drizzle of delicious virgin olive oil.
3. When the greens are golden brown, cover with the vegetable stock.
4. Crush the instruction with a touch of cream or milk cream and serve the new corn cream. Garnish with corn kernels and chopped parsley.

28. Keto Zucchini Cream

INGREDIENTS:
- 3-medium zucchini
- 1-onion
- 1-large potato
- ½ leek
- 200 ml of water
- 100 ml of cream or liquid cream
- 30 ml olive oil
- 1-tablet of chicken stock

DIRECTION:
1. Wash all vegetables.
2. Cut the zucchini, leek, onion, and potato into small cubes.
3. Heat the oil in a portion and fry the onion and leek. Add the zucchini and potato and cook for 5 minutes or until the zucchini starts to color.
4. Add a tablet of stock and a glass of water and cook the dinner for 20 minutes.
5. Remove from heat and mash the vegetables with the blender until you get a creamy texture. Finally, add the cream and mix— season with salt and ground black pepper.

29. Keto Pumpkin Cream Soup

INGREDIENTS:
- 1 pound pumpkin or pumpkin
- ¼ onion
- 2-butter spoons
- 2-tablespoons of flour
- 2-tablespoons of olive oil
- ¾ cups of cream or milk cream
- Toast
- 2-cups of chicken stock
- A handful of chopped fresh parsley and ground black pepper

DIRECTION:
1. Cut the pumpkin into pieces and remove the seeds and fibers by scraping them with a spoon.
2. Place the squash in a microwave-safe box and cook dinner for 10 minutes. Remove, and when it is soft, remove the skin and put the pulp in a blender along with the chicken stock. Blend until it is cut for miles. If you no longer have a microwave, don't worry now because you can chop the squash in water for dinner until it's cooked for miles or even baked.

3. Put the butter and oil in a pan, bring it to the fire when it is hot; add the peeled and finely chopped onion, and cook until transparent.
4. Season with salt and black pepper to taste and add the cream or milk cream. Cook for a few minutes. If the pumpkin cream soup is very thick, you can add water or chicken stock.
5. Serve the pumpkin cream soup on a deep plate or in bowls and decorate with

30. Keto Avocado Spring Rolls

INGREDIENTS:
- ¼-cup diced red onion
- 2-tablespoons chopped fresh cilantro leaves
- Juice 1 lime
- Kosher salt and freshly ground black pepper, to taste
- 1-cup vegetable oil
- 8-spring roll wrappers
- Cilantro Dipping Sauce
- ¾-cup fresh cilantro leaves, loosely packed
- ⅓-cup sour cream
- 1-jalapeño seeded and gutted (optional)
- 2-tablespoons mayonnaise
- 1-clove garlic

DIRECTIONS:
1. First, mix all INGREDIENTS for the cilantro dipping sauce and set it aside.
2. In a medium bowl, mash the avocados slightly with the back of a fork. Gently mix the tomato, onion, cilantro, lime juice, salt, and pepper.
3. Heat the oil in a deep skillet or saucepan over medium to high heat.

4. Grab your spring roll wrappers and fill them all with some avocado mixture. Fold the edges over and fold the top and bottom down. You can wet your fingers and dampen the packaging to seal the seams.
5. When the oil is heated, add the spring rolls and fry until beautifully golden brown. Then remove them and place them on a towel to drain.

31. Keto Sweetcorn Cakes

INGREDIENTS:
- 1-½-teaspoon granulated sugar
- ¼-teaspoon ground cumin
- ¼-teaspoon salt
- ⅛-teaspoon ground black pepper
- For the Pico De Gallo:
- 1-large Roma tomato, diced
- 1-tablespoon red onion, diced
- 1-tablespoon fresh cilantro, chopped
- ½-teaspoon lime juice
- Salt and ground pepper to taste
- For Southwestern Sauce:
- ½-cup mayonnaise
- 1-teaspoon white vinegar
- 1-teaspoon water
- ½-teaspoon granulated sugar
- ½-teaspoon chili powder

DIRECTIONS:
1. First, make the Salsa Verde. Pulse the INGREDIENTS for the Salsa Verde in the blender so that it is roughly combined.
2. Make the Pico de Gallo and Southwestern Sauce by mixing the INGREDIENTS when they are all well combined, cover them and put them in the fridge.

3. Prepare the corn cakes. First, place 1 cup of corn in the blender or kitchen appliance and puree.
4. Combine the mashed corn, butter, sugar, and salt in a medium bowl and mix.
5. In a small bowl, combine the masa and flour and stir. Add the remaining corn and masa mixture to the butter and corn mixture, mix well and shape into patties.

32. Keto Lasagna With Feta And Black Olives

INGREDIENTS:
- 600 gr tomato cubes
- Dried basil and oregano
- Salt and black pepper
- 1-sugar
- +/- 300 ml bechamel
- 1-jar of kalamata black olives without stone
- +/- 150 gr block feta
- A little grated cheese for browning

DIRECTIONS:
1. Heat a little olive oil in a saucepan or frying pan. Add the tomato cubes, sugar, dried basil and oregano, salt, and pepper (add to taste). Simmer for at least half an hour. Prepare your béchamel as usual. Drain the olives and cut the feta into cubes.
2. Spread a little tomato and béchamel sauce on the bottom of a gratin dish, place 2- sheets of lasagna, tomato sauce, béchamel, black olives, and diced feta. Continue in the same way until all the INGREDIENTS are used up. Finish with béchamel, sprinkle with grated cheese, and sprinkle with Greek herbs.

33. Baked Keto Cheese With Mushrooms

INGREDIENTS:
- 300 g of halloumi cheese
- 75 g butter 10-green olives
- salt and ground black pepper
- 125 ml (125 g) mayonnaise (optional)

DIRECTIONS:
1. Rinse, chop, and chop or slice the mushrooms.
2. Heat the right amount of butter in a pan to which they match and halloumi cheese and mushrooms.
3. Fry the mushrooms over medium heat for 3-5 minutes until golden brown. Salpimentarlos.

34. Keto Wings

INGREDIENTS:
- 2-cups of plain flour
- 1-teaspoon of garlic powder
- 1-teaspoon of chili pepper
- 1-teaspoon paprika or paprika
- 1-teaspoon of salt
- ½ teaspoon ground black pepper
- Half a bar of melted butter

DIRECTIONS:
1. The wings must be dry and completely thawed; skip them on a towel to shed all moisture. Mix the flour, salt, paprika, chili, garlic, and pepper and break the wings very well, let them rest in the fridge for at least an hour and then bake them again. If you want them without breadcrumbs, follow the same procedure; however, without flour, it is not essential to keep them in the fridge before deep-frying as they should be cooked longer so that the skin turns golden brown.
2. Heat the oil in a deep and massive pan or frying pan and fry the wings on each side until browned, without burning.

35. Keto Veggie Patch Pizza

INGREDIENTS:
- 4-lobster tails, fresh or thawed
- ¼ cup cold butter, sliced
- Salt and pepper
- Lemon wedges, to serve
- Preheat the grill and put a baking dish with foil.

DIRECTION:
1. Place the lobster tails with the shell on the cutting board one by one. Cut it open in the middle with kitchen scissors and spread it open. (You can remove part of the shell if you make this easier.) Separate the meat from the shell, but leave it in—season with salt and pepper.
2. Place the lobster tails in the baking dish and top with slices of butter.

36. Keto Pumpkin Cream With Edible Mushrooms

INGREDIENTS:

- 1-large pumpkin
- 500c.c. chicken bouillon
- 350 g edible mushrooms
- 100 g grated Parmesan cheese
- 1-onion
- 2-cloves of garlic
- A splash of liquid cream
- Salt and nutmeg c / n
- Olive oil c / n

DIRECTION:

1. Clean and peel the pumpkin.
2. Cut it in 1/2 and skip a peeled clove of garlic so that the pulp is infused with the flavor.
3. Put them on a tray; pour a little olive oil over the pumpkin and bake at 250 ° C for 60 minutes.
4. After this era, field the baked pumpkin in a pan with the bird stock and peeled onion; cook for 20 minutes.
5. When the squash is soft, crush everything in a blender.

6. Add some grated Parmesan cheese and continue to crush.
7. Place a few olive oils with the last clove of garlic peeled and chopped, and fry the rolled edible mushrooms. Keep the mushrooms when they are cooked.
8. Serve the pumpkin cream in soup dishes or clay stews with a little grated Parmesan cheese, salt, nutmeg, cream, and mushrooms.

37. Keto Creamy Tuscan Soup Olive Garden

INGREDIENTS:
- 1-pound spicy Italian ground says it can no longer be used for the first time
- 4-tablespoons of butter
- 1/2 cut into cubes
- 1-tablespoon of garlic
- 6-pieces of chicken bread
- 2-cups water
- 4/5 yellow potatoes, cut into 1-centimeter pieces
- 3-examples of salt or to taste
- 1-example blank pepper
- 2-cups in total
- 4-cups choppped kale
- chopped bacon or bacon bits and grated parmesan cheese for topping

DIRECTIONS:
1. In a larger stage, eat your sausage for 5-6 minutes until brown. Use a finished spoon to make an effort to get a plan and then try it.
2. Similarly, add a button and add another media dialog until it is translucent. Add some and let rest for another minute until fragrant.

3. Add some stock, water, potatoes, salt and cook it to a boil. Cook until they are different. Sneaky in kale and heavy. Add an example. Taste and fresh fruit and pepper, if necessary. Serve with some Parmesan cheese, if desired.

38. Keto Spinach Egg Soufflé

INGREDIENTS:
- 3-ways to start, thawed
- 3-tablespoons finely chopped
- 2-teaspoons can be used
- 1-teaspoon can turn into pepper
- 5-eggs
- 2-tablespoons milk
- 2-possible problems they've had
- 1/4 cup should be chosen
- 1/4 cup shredded Monterey Jack cheese
- 1-tablespoon grated Parmesan cheese
- 1/4 teaspoon of cream puffs

DIRECTIONS:
1. Preheat the oven to 375 ° F.
2. Combine spinach, artichoke hearts, onion, and purple bell pepper in a small bowl. Add 2-tablespoons of water, cover the bowl with plastic wrap, and put a few containers in the plastic - microwave over high heat for three minutes.

3. Beat four times. Mix in milk, cream, other cheese, Jack cheese, Parmesan, and salt. Indeed, in the story, in the first place, on and in the bubble pepper. Mix the egg aggregate at a high temperature for 30 seconds and then stir it. Do this 4 to 5 more times or until you have a very runny scrambled egg mixture. With this procedure, the eggs are stretched enough so that the dough does not sink into the eggs while also filling.
4. Roll out and rate the new rectangles. Make sure you don't differ the dough from the goal that makes triangles. Instead, compare the work together next to the diagonal perforations so that you have 4-rectangles.

39. Keto Copycat Eggplant Cannelloni

INGREDIENTS:
- 250 g hake fillets without skin or bones
- 250 g shrimp tails
- 50 g grated cheese
- 2-medium eggplants 1-pack of cannelloni
- 1-tablet of chicken stock
- bechamel
- 2-peppers

DIRECTION:
1. Wash the aubergines and let them reduce lengthwise. Place them on a baking tray and drizzle with a drizzle of oil.
2. Bake the aubergines at 200 ° C for 20 minutes.
3. Soak the cannelloni, and when they are well hydrated, remove and dry with a cloth.
4. Fry the fish and shrimps with a dash of oil and season with the bird stock.
5. Chop hake fillets, shrimp, peppers, and the flesh of the aubergines you roasted. Mix with tablespoons of béchamel sauce and fill the cannelloni.

6. Place the aubergine cannelloni on a plate and cover it with béchamel sauce. Sprinkle with grated cheese and gratin.

40. Keto yummy Pasta With Mushrooms

INGREDIENTS:
- 250 g mushrooms
- 5 g chopped fresh parsley
- 3-spring onions
- 1-onion
- 1-tablespoon of mustard
- 2-tablespoons of olive, sunflower, or corn oil

DIRECTION:
1. Put much water in a saucepan in addition to a little oil and salt. Cook the pasta al dente and drain.
2. Thinly slice the green onions next to the appropriate mushrooms. Halve the cherry tomatoes and the onion in pen. In a non-stick frying pan, sauté the spring onions and regular onion with a little oil and when the onion is translucent, add the mushrooms and cook for dinner until golden brown.
3. Mix the cream or milk cream with the mustard and heat in a pan. Add the cherry tomatoes to the pan, which you had to reduce in half, and finally, add the cooked and drained pasta along with the onions.
4. Heat for a few seconds and serve in dishes.

5. Garnish with chopped fresh parsley and season.

Conclusion

Lastly, I would like to thank you for choosing this book. These recipes are most beneficial for pregnant women and women during pregnancy can easily maintain their Keto diet schedule by eating these meals which are low in carb and delicious as well. Good luck!

Keto recipes for women over 50

Table of Contents

INTRODUCTION

Ketogenic diet can be adopted in any age. Ketones are at the point of convergence of the ketogenic diet. You can get more slender On after Keto meals. Your body produces ketones, a fuel molecule, as an elective fuel source when the body is missing the mark on glucose. Making ketones happens when you decline carb permit and eat up the ideal proportion of protein. Right when you're eating Keto very much arranged food assortments, your liver can move muscle versus fat into ketones, which by then get used as a fuel source by your body. When the body is using fat for a fuel source, you're in ketosis. This allows the body to grow its fat devouring radically sometimes, which assists with reducing pockets of unfortunate fat. Not solely does this method for fat devouring help you with getting fit as a fiddle, anyway it can in like manner turn away desires and thwart energy crashes for the term of the day. That's why women over 50 can also follow ketogenic diet schedule and have low carb delicious meals.

41. Coconut Curry Cauliflower Soup

YIELDS: 4 PREP TIME: 0 HOURS 5 MINS TOTAL TIME: 0 HOURS 35 MINS

INGREDIENTS

- 1/4 c. pepitas, toasted
- 1 tsp. Additional virgin olive oil
- 2 garlic cloves, chopped
- 1 tsp. new ginger, stripped and chopped
- 1 c. yellow onion, chopped
- 1 c. carrots, chopped
- 1 tsp. legitimate salt
- 1 huge cauliflower head, cut into florets
- 32 oz. low-sodium vegetable stock

- 1 c. full-fat coconut milk (shake well ahead of time)
- 2 tbsp. red curry paste
- 1/4 c. new cilantro, chopped
- Flaky ocean salt

DIRECTIONS

1. In a little skillet, dry toast pepitas on low heat until brilliant brown, around 2 minutes. Put in a safe spot.
2. In an enormous pot over medium-low heat, heat olive oil. Add garlic, ginger, onion, carrots, and salt. Cook for 5 minutes.
3. Add cauliflower, stock, coconut milk, and curry paste. Mix well, heat to the point of boiling, and afterward stew for 20 minutes. Mix with a drenching blender until smooth.

42. Lemon Black Pepper Tuna Salad Recipe

Prep Time: 10 minutes | Cooking Time: 0 minutes | Yield: 1 serving

INGREDIENTS:

- 1/3 cucumber, cut into small cubes
- 1/2 small avocado, cut into small cubes
- 1 teaspoon of lemon juice
- 1 can (100-150 g) of tuna
- 1 tablespoon Paleo mayo (use olive oil for AIP)
- 1 tablespoon mustard (omit for AIP)
- Salt to taste
- Salad greens (optional)
- Black pepper to taste (omit AIP)

DIRECTIONS:

1. Mix the diced cucumber and avocado with the lemon juice.
2. Peel the tuna and mix well with the mayo and mustard.
3. Add the tuna to the avocado and cucumber. Add salt to taste.
4. Prepare the green salads (optional: add olive oil and lemon juice to taste).
5. Place the tuna salad on top of the green lettuce.
6. Sprinkle with black pepper.

43. Keto Avocado Fudge Cookies

*Prep time: 5 minutes | Resting time: 5 minutes | C
ALSO time: 12 minutes*

INGREDIENTS:

- 100 grams of ripe avocado
- 1 large egg
- 1/2 cup of unsweetened cocoa powder
- 1/4 cup unsweetened shredded coconut
- 1/4 cup of erythritol
- 1/2 teaspoon of baking powder
- 3/8 tsp. liquid stevia
- 1/4 teaspoon of pink Himalayan salt

DIRECTIONS:

1. Preheat your oven to 350 degrees F and line a baking sheet with parchment paper.

2. Cut the avocado into the skin and place it in a large mixing bowl. Puree as much as possible with a fork.

3. Add the egg, erythritol, stevia and salt and mix with a hand mixer to a uniform consistency.

4. Add the cocoa, coconut flakes and baking powder and mix again.

5. Scoop 9 cookies onto the baking tray with a cookie scoop. Use a spoon or your finger to spread the cookies out to the desired size.

6. Optionally, cover with lily of chocolate or abraded baker chocolate. Bake for 10-12 minutes, until set.

7. Let cool for five minutes before using.

8. Best store in a zip-lock bag in the refrigerator for up to a week. To enjoy!

44. Keto Breaded fish recipe (with cod)

Prep time: 10 minutes | Cooking time: 20 minutes | Yield: 4 servings

INGREDIENTS:

- 4 cod fillets (about 0.3 lb. each) (or use other fish)
- 1/2 cup of coconut flour
- 2 tablespoons of coconut flakes
- 3 tablespoons of garlic powder
- 1 tablespoon of onion powder
- Salt to taste
- 2 tablespoons of ghee
- 3 cloves of garlic, chopped
- Coconut oil for greasing baking tray

DIRECTIONS:

1. Preheat the oven to 425F (220C).
2. In a large bowl, combine the breading (coconut flour, coconut flakes, garlic powder, and onion powder). Add salt and taste the mixture to see how much salt you like.
3. Cover a baking tray with aluminum foil and grease with coconut oil .
4. Dip each fish fillet in the breading mixture and cover well. Place the breaded fish on the baking tray.
5. Bake for 15-20 minutes until the fish flakes easily.
6. While the fish is in the oven, prepare the garlic ghee sauce   by melting the ghee a little and adding the chopped garlic.
7. Pour the garlic ghee sauce over the breaded fish and serve.

45. Keto Low Carb Oven Baked Fish

Preparation Time: 25 mins |Cooking Time: 20 mins
|Total Time: 45 mins | Servings: 4

INGREDIENTS:

- For breading
- For the eggs
- For the fish
- For the pan

DIRECTIONS:

1. To Prepare: Preheat the oven to 430 ° F. Add a dark colored pan or baking tray to the oven while it heats up - the pan you want to bake the fish in must be hot to melt the butter!

2. Making breadcrumbs: Mix all of them for the breading in a shallow bowl.

3. Preparing eggs: Add the eggs to a SEPARATE shallow dish and beat well.

4. Bread fish: Dip the fish in breadcrumbs to lightly coat it. Then cover the fish with egg. FINALLY, cover the fish with breadcrumbs again, this time you can really grab as much as it sticks! (Just put the breaded pieces of fish on a plate until you've breaded them all.)

5. Melting butter: Take the pan out of the oven VERY CAREFULLY. Add 3 tablespoons of butter to the pan to melt. Divide over the pan and place the pieces of fish on top.

6. Baking: fry the fish for 10 minutes. Flip, add remaining 1 tablespoon butter and cook for 5-10 minutes or until coating are crisp and fish is cooked through.

7. Finish: grill for 2 minutes for a crispy coating. After cooking, let the fish rest on the pan for 2-3 minutes and serve immediately.

46. Keto Curry Bowl With Spinach

Preparation Time: 5 mins |Cooking Time: 10 mins |
Total Time: 15 mins| Servings: 4 | Net
Carbohydrates: 4g

INGREDIENTS:

DIRECTIONS:

1. Gently fry the sliced onion in coconut oil until the onion is cooked and clear.
2. Add the garlic and curry powder, stir and cook for another minute. Be careful not to burn the garlic.
3. Add the ground beef / mince and keep stirring until well cooked.
4. Add the coconut cream and stir.

5. While the curried beef is still simmering in the pan, start adding the chopped spinach a handful at a time. Stir the spinach into the curried beef so that it softens. Repeat until all of the spinach has been added.

6. Serve the Keto curry in bowls and enjoy! Garnish with coconut cream (optional).

47. Keto Chili Recipe

Preparation Time: 10 mins |Cooking Time: 1 hour |
Total Time: 1 hour 10 mins| Yield: 6 Servings

INGREDIENTS:

- 1 ½ pounds ground beef
- 1 yellow onion, diced
- 1 green pepper, diced
- 1 jalapeno, finely chopped
- 1 clove of garlic, finely chopped
- ¼ cup of tomato paste
- 15 ounces of canned diced tomatoes
- 2 cups of beef stock
- 2 tablespoons chili powder
- 1 teaspoon of cumin
- 1 teaspoon of salt

DIRECTIONS:

1. Add the ground beef, onion, and bell pepper to a large deep pan and cook over medium heat, breaking the meat into pieces while cooking. Drain the fat from the pan when the meat is cooked.

2. Add the jalapeno, garlic, tomato paste, diced tomatoes, beef stock, chili powder, cumin and salt and stir.

3. Bring to a boil and simmer. Simmer for a minimum of 20 minutes, preferably an hour for the best flavor and texture.

4. Serve with sour cream and grated cheddar, as desired

48. Easy Keto Hamburger Casserole Recipe

Prep Time 15 mins Cook Time 30 mins Total Time 45 mins

INGREDIENTS

- 1½ pounds ground beef see tips below
- 2 tablespoons olive oil plus more for the pan
- 1 teaspoon onion powder
- 1 teaspoon garlic powder
- 1 teaspoon Dijon mustard
- 1 tablespoon tomato paste sugar-free – see tips below
- ½ teaspoon ground pepper
- 1 teaspoon salt
- 3 eggs
- ½ cup heavy cream
- 1½ cups cheddar grated

- 3 cups green beans canned or frozen – see tips below

DIRECTIONS:

1. Oil an 8×8" baking dish with olive oil and set aside. Preheat your oven to 360°F. Put 1½ pounds ground beef, 1 teaspoon onion powder, 1 teaspoon garlic powder, 1 teaspoon Dijon mustard, 1 tablespoon tomato paste, ½ teaspoon ground pepper, and 1 teaspoon salt in a large bowl. Stir well until mixed.
2. Ground beef and other INGREDIENTS in a glass bowl for Keto hamburger casserole
3. Heat 2 tablespoons olive oil in a large skillet. Add the ground beef paste and cook for about 10 minutes, breaking it up as it cooks, until it browns completely.
4. Browning the ground beef in a skillet
5. Add the cooked ground beef mixture to your prepared baking dish in an even layer. Blowout 3 cups canned or frozen green beans over the beef.
6. Green beans on top of beef for Keto casserole recipe

7. In a medium bowl, beat 3 eggs. Add ½ cup heavy cream and a pinch of salt. Evenly pour this mixture over the meat and green beans. Spread 1½ cups grated cheese over the top of the beef and green bean mixture.

8. Adding cheese to Keto casserole recipe

9. Then bake for 20-30 minutes, until the cheese is golden brown. Present, and enjoy!

10. Serving of Keto casserole recipe on a plate with a baking dish of hamburger casserole

11. Notes

12. Mix with ground pork: You can use ground pork in addition to beef for even more flavor. Use a mixture of 1 pound ground beef and 5 ounces ground pork if you would like to use pork.

13. Sugar-free tomato paste: Make sure your tomato paste is sugar-free. You can substitute it with sugar-free ketchup.

14. Using frozen green beans: If using frozen green beans, you do not need to thaw them. They will cook completely when baking the casserole.

15. Other veggies to use: Not a fan of green beans? You can still make this easy Keto

hamburger recipe! Try using cauliflower or broccoli instead. Broccoli is one of our personal favorites!

49. Easy Pork Crawler Recipe With Vegetables (Low Carb)

Cooking Time: 5 mins | Total Time: 15 mins|
Servings: 4 | Calories: 266kcal

INGREDIENTS:

- 3/4-pound pork loin, cut into thin strips
- 2 tablespoons avocado or olive oil (divided)
- 1 tablespoon of fresh ground ginger
- 1 teaspoon of chopped garlic
- 12 ounces of broccoli florets
- 1 red pepper, cut into strips
- 1 bunch green onions (scallions), in pieces of 2-inch cut
- 2 tablespoons Tamari soy sauce (or coconut aminos)
- 1 tablespoon of extra dry sherry

- 1 1/2 tablespoons low-carb sugar (or sugar or coconut sugar)
- 1 teaspoon cornstarch (or arrowroot)
- 1 teaspoon of sesame oil

DIRECTIONS:

1. Preparation: Finely chop a clove of garlic. Cut a 2.5 cm piece of ginger and peel the thin skin with a spoon. Finely chop the ginger and add it to the garlic. Cut the pork tenderloin into thin strips and mix with 1 tbsp. oil and the ginger and garlic.

2. Cut the red pepper into strips and place in the bottom of a medium bowl. Cut the green onions (scallions) into 2-inch pieces, including some of the green stems, and add them to the bowl. Cut the broccoli florets into large, bite-sized pieces and place on top.

3. Add the sweetener and cornstarch (arrowroot) to a small bowl and mix. Stir in Tamari soy sauce, dry sherry and sesame oil.

4. Method: Put the wok on high heat. It is ready when a drop of water jumps over the surface. Add 1 tablespoon of oil and quickly tilt the wok to cover all surfaces. Pour out the remaining oil. Return the wok to the heat and add the pork to the sides and bottom of the pan. Leave the pork alone until it is cooked through halfway through the cooking time; the bottom half turns white. Stir the pork and cook until almost done. Remove from pan to serving bowl.

5. Dump the bowl of vegetables into the wok with the broccoli on the bottom. Cover with a lid and cook for 1 minute. Stir the vegetables and return the pork and any juices to the pan. Stir the pork and vegetables together. Stir in the stir-fry sauce and pour it over the pork and vegetables. Move the pork stir-fry aside and let the sauce cook in the bottom of the wok, stirring occasionally for a few seconds until the sauce thickens.

6. If you want the sauce to be thicker, remove the stir-fried pork and vegetables from the serving bowl and let the sauce cook a little longer. When the sauce has reached the desired consistency, pour the sauce over the stir-fry. Serve.

50. Keto Stuffed Pork Tenderloin with Mushroom Sauce

Preparation Time: 10 mins |Cooking Time: 40 mins |
Total Time: 40mins| Yield: 4

INGREDIENTS:

- 1 pound of pork tenderloin
- 2 tablespoons of oil
- 3 slices of provolone cheese
- 1/3 cup of freshly chopped spinach
- salt and pepper to taste
- 1 teaspoon of crushed garlic
- 8 oz. mushrooms sliced
- 1 tablespoon of balsamic vinegar
- 1 large clove of garlic, finely chopped
- 2 tablespoons of butter

- 1 teaspoon better than stock beef mixed with 1 cup of water (or 1 cup of beef stock)
- 1 tablespoon of whipped cream

DIRECTIONS:

1. Preheat the oven to 375 degrees F.
2. Cut the pork tenderloin lengthwise but leave 1/2 inch so you can open it like a book.
3. Wrap the meat in plastic and pound thinly to about 1/4 - 1/2 inches thick.
4. Sprinkle chopped garlic and salt and pepper over the meat.
5. Layer the cheese slices and then the spinach.
6. Roll up tightly lengthwise and secure with string or toothpicks.
7. Heat oil in a pan and fry the meat for about 5 minutes on each side.
8. Put in the oven and cook for about 25 minutes.
9. In the meantime, add butter and mushrooms to a large sauté pan and cook for about 5 minutes.
10. Add the garlic and stock and cook for another 5 minutes until slightly reduced.

11. Add the vinegar and mix well. Then add the cream and mix.

12. When the meat comes out of the oven, let it stand for 10 minutes and then pour mushroom sauce over it.

51. Cheesy Keto Meatball Casserole

Preparation Time: 5 mins |Cooking Time: 40 mins |
Total Time: 45 mins

INGREDIENTS:

- For the meatballs:

- 2 pounds of ground beef
- 1/2 cup of grated Parmesan cheese
- 3/4 cup shredded mozzarella cheese
- 1 egg
- 1/4 cup of grated onion
- 3 cloves of garlic, chopped
- 3 tablespoons of chopped fresh parsley
- 1/2 teaspoon onion powder
- 1/2 teaspoon garlic powder
- 1/2 teaspoon of Italian seasoning

- Salt and pepper to taste
- For the frying pan:

- 1 (24 oz.) jar of favorite marinara sauce (I prefer Rao's)
- 1/2 cup of ricotta cheese
- 1/2 cup of grated mozzarella cheese
- 2 to 3 tablespoons of fresh basil, chopped

DIRECTIONS:

1. Preheat the oven to 400 degrees F.
2. To make the meatballs: Combine ground beef, cheese, egg, onion, garlic, parsley and herbs in a large bowl and mix well. Use a cookie spoon to shape the meatballs so that they are all the same size, roll them around in your hands and place on a baking dish or baking tray. You should get about 15 to 16 large meatballs.
3. Bake meatballs for 20 to 25 minutes, or until cooked through. Remove meatballs, drain excess fat and place cooked meatballs in a baking dish.

4. Pour the marinara sauce evenly over the meatballs and spoon over the ricotta cheese. Sprinkle with mozzarella cheese and bake in the oven for about 15 minutes until the cheese is melted and bubbly.

5. Remove from oven and cover with fresh basil. Serve and enjoy!

52. Keto Curry Bowl With Spinach

Prep Time: 5 minutes Cook Time: 10 minutes Total Time: 15 minutes Servings: 4 NET carbs: 4g

INGREDIENTS

- 1 onion sliced
- 2 cloves garlic
- 2 tbsp. curry powder
- 750 g (1.7 lb.) ground/minced beef
- 125 ml (0.5 cups) coconut cream
- 6 cups spinach chopped finely

DIRECTIONS:

1. Slightly fry the sliced onion in coconut oil until the onion is cooked and clear.

2. Then add the garlic and curry powder stir and cook for another minute. Be careful not to allow the garlic to burn.

3. Add the ground/minced beef and endure to stir until thoroughly cooked.

4. Add the coconut cream and stir.

5. At the same time as the curried beef is still simmering in the pan, begin to add the chopped spinach one handful at a time. Stir the spinach through the curried beef so it wilts. Repeat until all the spinach is added.

6. Present the Keto curry in bowls, and enjoy! Garnish with coconut cream (optional).

53. Keto Wonton Soup with shrimps

Prep Time: 1 HOUR Cook Time: 5 MINUTES Total Time: 1 HOUR 5 MINUTES Servings: 8 servings

INGREDIENTS

- 1 pack wonton coverings (80 coverings)
- Filling
- 1/2 lbs. (230 g) ground lean pork
- 1/2 lbs. (230 g) stripped shrimp, chopped into little pieces
- 1 tablespoon finely minced ginger
- 2 green onions , finely chopped
- 1 tablespoon light soy sauce (or soy sauce)
- 2 tablespoons Shaoxing wine (or dry sherry)

- 1/2 teaspoon salt
- 2 tablespoons sesame oil
- (Alternative 1) Chicken soup base
- 8 cups chicken stock
- 8 teaspoons light soy sauce (or soy sauce)
- 8 teaspoons minced ginger
- 8 teaspoons sesame oil
- Salt , to taste
- (Choice 2) Chinese road style soup base
- 8 cups hot stock from the wonton bubbling water
- 8 tablespoons papery dried shrimp , or to taste
- 8 major bits of dried ocean growth for soup , arranged by guidance (*Footnote 1)
- 4 teaspoons chicken bouillon
- 8 teaspoons light soy sauce , or to taste
- 8 teaspoons sesame oil
- Garnishes
- 4 green onions , chopped
- 4 stalks infant bok choy , slice to reduced down (or 4 cups infant spinach)
- 1 bunch cilantro, chopped (Optional)
- Hand crafted stew oil , to taste (Optional)

DIRECTIONS

1. Make the filling

2. Without a food processor: Combine ground pork, shrimp, ginger, green onion, soy sauce, Shaoxing wine, salt and sesame oil in a major bowl. Blend well in with a fork until everything consolidates well together and the combination feels somewhat tacky.

3. With a food processor or a blender: coarsely cleave the ginger and green onion. Add all the filling INGREDIENTS with the exception of the shrimp. Blend until it frames a velvety paste. Add the shrimp and mix once more, until the shrimp are finely chopped however don't turn into a paste.

4. Wrap the wonton

5. To make wontons, place a wonton covering in one hand, scoop a teaspoon of wonton filling and spot it close to the restricted side of the wonton covering (you can add more filling to the wonton on the off chance that you like, as long as you can in any case wrap it). Overlap the restricted side over the filling; at that point roll the filling right through the opposite side of

the covering. Tie the two finishes and press together to bolt the filling inside the covering. Brush a dainty layer of water onto the wonton covering and press the closures together.

6. Make each wonton in turn, and line up every one of the wontons on a major wooden cutting board. In the event that you're not going to heat up the wontons promptly, utilize a moist paper towel (or cheesecloth) to cover the wontons to keep them from drying out.

7. On the off chance that you're not going to heat up the wontons that very day, place them in a water/air proof holder with a few layers of wet paper towels on the base. Thusly, they can be put away in the cooler for as long as 2 days.

8. (Alternative 1) Make the chicken soup base

9. Consolidate the chicken stock, ginger, and soy sauce in a pot. Heat to the point of boiling. Let bubble for 10 minutes. Go to least heat to keep warm and begin cooking wontons (see beneath).

10. Plan 8 medium-sized dishes. Add the cooked wontons and bok choy. Add 2 tablespoons green onion, 1 tablespoon soy sauce and 1/2 teaspoon sesame oil into each bowl. Pour in 1

and 1/2 cups hot stock. Trimming with cilantro and stew oil, if using.

11. Serve hot.

12. (Alternative 2) Make the road seller style soup base

13. To get ready 1 serving of wonton soup base, add a major spoon of cilantro, 1 tablespoon papery dried shrimps, a liberal piece of dried kelp, 1/4 teaspoon chicken bouillon, and some child bok choy into a major bowl. Rehash the interaction to set up the remainder of the soup base in the other serving bowls. Cook wontons (see beneath).

14. To make 1 serving of wonton soup, utilize a spoon to move cooked wontons, bok choy, and the hot soup into a serving bowl with every one of the INGREDIENTS from the past advance. Sprinkle 1 teaspoon soy sauce and 1 teaspoon sesame oil into the bowl and give it a delicate mix. The soup ought to be golden hued. Add additional soy sauce or salt if the soup isn't sufficiently pungent. Dissipate green onion on top. Enhancement with cilantro and stew oil, if using.

15. Serve hot.

16. Heated up the wonton

17. To heat up the wontons, heat a major pot of water until bubbling. Add 10 to 20 wontons all at once and bubble over medium heat until wontons are drifting on the outside of the water. Keep on bubbling until the coverings are swollen, around 1 to 2 minutes for little wontons and 2 to 3 minutes for greater ones. Take a wonton out with an opened spoon and split it with a chopstick or fork. On the off chance that the wonton is cooked through, stop heat quickly and move the wontons to singular serving bowls. If not, keep on bubbling until cooked through.

18. Whenever you've cooked the wontons, add the bok choy. Let cook until delicate. Eliminate from the pot, channel well, and put in a safe spot.

19. To cook frozen wontons

20. Heat a huge pot of water to the point of boiling over high heat. Add wontons. Mix tenderly to keep from staying. Cook until heating the water to the point of boiling once more. Go to medium-low heat. Cover the pot with a little hole on one side, to forestall spilling. Keep

bubbling for 2 minutes (3 minutes for bigger wontons). Remain adjacent to the pot the entire chance to screen the stock. On the off chance that the stock begins to spill, reveal and mix, and supplant the cover. Uncover and keep cooking for one more moment, or until the wontons are cooked through.

21. There are numerous kinds of dried ocean growth. My unique formula utilized a sort of moment ocean growth that will rehydrate quickly once positioned into the hot soup. There are different kinds of fish that require some splashing prior to using. Peruse the rear of your bundle and adhere to the guidelines as needs be.

22. The sustenance realities for this formula are determined dependent on 1 bowl of chicken-stock based soup containing 10 wontons.

54. Keto Beef Meal

Preparation Time: 15 mins |Cooking Time: 30 mins |
Total Time: 45 mins| Servings: 5

INGREDIENTS:

- 2 pounds of ground beef
- 2 teaspoons fresh parsley and mint chopped
- 1.5 teaspoons smoked paprika and cumin
- ¼ teaspoon of cayenne pepper
- 2 cloves of garlic grated
- ½ teaspoon of dried thyme
- Peel ½ lemon
- Kosher salt and black pepper
- Avocado or grape seed oil
- ¾ cup of full-fat Greek yogurt
- 1 teaspoon fresh parsley and mint chopped
- Peel of half a lemon

- 1 tablespoon of lemon juice
- 1 clove of garlic
- 1 teaspoon of extra virgin olive oil
- Kosher salt and black pepper
- 2 medium zucchinis of about 12 grams
- ½ head of cauliflower
- 1 pound broccoli with stalks or 12 ounces florets
- ½ onion chopped
- 2 cloves of garlic finely chopped
- 1 teaspoon of mustard seeds
- ¼ teaspoon of red pepper flakes
- 1 teaspoon fresh parsley and mint chopped
- Peel and juice from half a lemon
- 2 tablespoons chopped pecans toasted if desired
- Kosher salt and black pepper
- Avocado or grape seed oil

DIRECTIONS:

1. Cook's notes: Watch the video in this post to learn how to cut the zucchini, cauliflower, and broccoli for the pilaf. Everything is cut small and similar in size, so they cook evenly.

2. Make the pilaf by chopping the zucchini, cauliflower, and broccoli into small pieces that are about the same size, being careful not to use too much of the stems. Preheat a large and wide pan over medium heat for 2 minutes. Add 2 teaspoons of oil to the pan, then the onions, garlic, mustard seeds, red pepper flakes, ¼ teaspoon of salt, and a few cracks of pepper.

3. Mix well and cook for 6 minutes, stirring often. Add the chopped zucchini, cauliflower, and broccoli to the pan along with ½ teaspoon of salt and a few cracks of pepper. Mix well and put a lid on the pan; you can also use a baking tray to cover the pan if you don't have a lid.

4. Cook for 10-12 minutes, stirring a few times. The vegetables are ready when they have softened but still have a bite. Reduce heat and add parsley, mint, lemon zest and juice, and pecans, tossing well. Check for herbs; you may need more lemon juice or salt. Put aside.

5. Add to rounds kefta the beef to a large bowl with the remaining (not oil), 1 teaspoon salt, and a few cracked peppers. Use your hands to mix everything very well. Shape the kefta by taking some of the meat and shaping it like a block of wood or football; watch the video to see how. You have enough beef to 14-15 kefta make.

6. Preheat a large pan, preferably cast iron, over medium heat for 2 minutes. Add 2 teaspoons of oil to the pan, wait 30 seconds for the oil to heat up, and then add half of the kefta to the pan. Cook for 3-4 minutes, or until well browned, flip and cook for another 3-4 minutes. If both sides are brown, you may need to cook the kefta on the sides for 30 seconds to cook them all the way through.

7. If you are not sure if the kefta is cooked, cut one in half and check that it is important not to overcook the kefta, or they will dry out. Remove kefta from the pan, add a little more oil and cook the second batch. While the kefta is cooking, make the yogurt sauce by combining everything in a bowl and whipping well. Check for herbs and adjust if necessary.

8. Serve the kefta with some yogurt sauce and pilaf; enjoy! Everything will keep in the fridge for 5 days, you can freeze the kefta for 2-3 months, but I would not recommend freezing the vegetables as they become very soft and watery. The best way to kefta and vegetables to warm up, 10 minutes in an oven at 400 F; if you use a microwave, cover the container or with a wet paper towel and make sure it does not overheat because of the meat from drying out.

55. Spinach Artichoke Dip Recipe

*Preparation Time: 10 mins |Cooking Time: 30 mins
|Total Time: 40 mins*

INGREDIENTS:

- 4 oz. Spinach (chopped)
- 4 oz. cream cheese
- 2 tablespoons of mayonnaise
- 2 tablespoons sour cream (or an additional 2 tablespoons mayonnaise)
- 1/4 cup of grated Parmesan cheese
- 1 can (14.5 oz.) artichoke hearts in water (drained, chopped, and pressed to release extra moisture)
- 4 cloves of garlic (finely chopped)
- 1/4 teaspoon black pepper

- 2/3 cup mozzarella cheese (shredded, divided into 2 parts)

DIRECTIONS:

1. Heat a greased pan over medium heat. Add the chopped spinach. Cook, stirring occasionally, until the spinach is limp and bright green. (You can also simmer the spinach in the microwave for 2-3 minutes.) Set aside to cool. If you want to speed up the cooling, you can place the bowl in a larger bowl of ice (optional).
2. While the spinach is cooling, preheat the oven to 350 degrees F (177 degrees C).
3. Meanwhile, heat the cream cheese in the microwave or in a small saucepan on the stove over low heat. Once it has melted enough to stir, add the mayonnaise, sour cream, grated Parmesan, chopped artichoke hearts, chopped garlic, black pepper, and half of the grated mozzarella. Stir to combine.

4. When the spinach is cool enough to handle, gather it into a ball and squeeze it a few times, making sure to get as much water out as possible. Add the spinach to the artichoke mixture.
5. Transfer the dip to a small ceramic appetizer dish or large bowl. Smooth the top with a spatula. Sprinkle with the remaining grated mozzarella.
6. Bake for about 30 minutes, until warm and bubbly. Serve warm.

56. Keto Stuffed Meatballs Cheese

Preparation Time: 10 mins |Cooking Time: 24 mins |Yield: 18 meats | Total Time: 34 mins|

INGREDIENTS:

- 1 pound ground beef (I get grass-fed ground beef from Butcher Box)
- 1 pound of Italian sausage
- 1 teaspoon of black pepper
- 1 teaspoon of dried oregano
- 1 teaspoon of garlic powder
- 3 mozzarella cheese sticks, cut into 1-inch pieces
- 2 tablespoons of avocado oil
- 1 jar low-carb marinara sauce (Mezzetta has an option for 6 cars per serving)

- 1 cup of low-fat, low-moisture mozzarella cheese
- 1 tablespoon parsley, chopped (for garnish)

DIRECTIONS:

1. In a large mixing bowl, combine ground beef, Italian sausage, salt, black pepper, dried oregano, and garlic powder.
2. Pour avocado oil into an oven-safe pan, making sure the entire bottom of the pan is covered with oil.
3. Grab about 1/4 cups (give or take some) of the meat mixture and put in a piece of the mozzarella cheese, then roll it into a ball. Place the meatball in the prepared ovenproof pan. Repeat until the meat is finished.
4. Set the oven to Grill and place the pan in the oven for about 12 minutes, or until the meatballs turn a nice golden brown on top.
5. Remove the pan from the oven and pour the marinara sauce over the meatballs. Then sprinkle the mozzarella cheese on top.

6. Return the pan to the oven and turn the oven to Bake at 350 degrees and bake for an additional 12 minutes, or until the internal temperature of the meatballs reaches 160 degrees.
7. Carefully remove the pan from the oven and garnish with chopped parsley.

57. Keto Asparagus Fries

Preparation Time: 20 mins |Cooking Time: 10 mins |Rest Time: 30 mins | Total Time: 1 hour

INGREDIENTS:

- 1 pound asparagus trimmed (thick if possible)
- Salt and pepper to taste
- 1 cup of Parmesan cheese
- 3/4 cup of almond flour
- 1/4 teaspoon of cayenne pepper
- 1/4 teaspoon baking powder
- 4 beaten eggs
- Oil spray I used avocado oil

DIRECTIONS:

1. Prick the asparagus with a fork. Season with at least 1/2 teaspoon of salt. Place them on kitchen paper and let them stand for 30 minutes.

2. Meanwhile, combine 1 cup of Parmesan cheese, almond flour, cayenne, and baking powder in a bowl. Season with salt and pepper. (I use 1/4 tsp. each.)

3. Beat the egg in a separate bowl.

4. Dip the asparagus in the eggs and cover with the cheese mixture.

5. Preheat your air fryer to 400 degrees.

6. Arrange the asparagus in a single layer and cook in batches if necessary. Spray well with oil. Let it boil for 5 minutes. Turnover and spray again. Cook another 4 to 5 minutes, until the asparagus is tender.

7. Fried Asparagus Fries

8. Preheat and oven to 420 degrees. Cover a baking tray with parchment paper.

9. Arrange the asparagus in a single layer. Spray with oil. Bake for 15 to 20 minutes.

58. Keto Shrimp Guacamole and Bacon

Preparation Time: 20 mins |Cooking Time: 20 mins
|Total Time: 40 mins | Servings: 20 | Calories:
60kcal

INGREDIENTS:

- For the Guacamole:

- 2 small avocados
- 1/2 cup chopped red onion
- 1/2 lime, squeezed
- 1/3 cup of fresh cilantro lightly packed
- 1/2 teaspoon of salt
- For the shrimp:

- 10 ounces of large raw shrimp, peeled and gutted, yield 20 shrimp
- 1/2 teaspoon of salt
- 1/4 teaspoon of pepper
- 1/2 teaspoon of cumin
- 2 tablespoons of butter

DIRECTIONS:

1. Make the Guacamole
2. Add all for the guacamole to a food processor and pulse until combined.
3. You want the guacamole to be a little thick. Taste for spices and adjust to your taste.
4. Boil the shrimp
5. Season both sides of the shrimp with salt, pepper and cumin.
6. Heat the butter in a large skillet over medium heat.
7. Sear the shrimp on both sides until they are no longer opaque.
8. Remove the pan from the heat and set aside.
9. Place the cucumber slices on a plate and season with salt.

10. Top with a slice of bacon, followed by a spoonful of guacamole.
11. Finish with a shrimp and secure with a toothpick.

59. Keto Beef and Broccoli

Preparation Time: 10 mins |Cooking Time: 25 mins |
Total Time: 35 mins| Calories: 294kcal

INGREDIENTS:

- 1 pound flank steak cut into 1/4-inch-thick strips
- 5 cups of small broccoli florets about 7 ounces
- 1 tablespoon of avocado oil
- 1 yellow onion sliced
- 1 tablespoon of butter
- ½ tbsp. olive oil
- 1/3 cup of low-sodium soy sauce
- ⅓ cup of beef stock
- 1 tablespoon of fresh ginger finely chopped
- 2 cloves of garlic finely chopped

DIRECTIONS:

1. Heat avocado oil in a pan over medium heat for a few minutes or until hot.
2. Add sliced beef and cook until brown, less than 5 minutes, don't stir too much, you want it to brown. Place on a plate and set aside.
3. Add onions to a skillet with butter and olive oil and cook for 20 minutes until onions are caramelized and tender.
4. Add all other sauce to the pan and stir the together over medium heat until it begins to simmer for about 5 minutes.
5. Use a hand blender to mix sauce.
6. Keep the sauce warm on low heat and add broccoli to the pan.
7. Return the beef to the pan and toss with the broccoli and sauce. Stir until covered with the sauce.
8. Bring to a boil and cook for a few more minutes until the broccoli is tender.
9. Season with salt and pepper, if necessary.
10. Serve immediately, possibly in combination with boiled cauliflower rice.

60. Keto Parmesan Roasted Broccoli

Total Time Prep/Total Time: 30 min. Makes 4 servings

INGREDIENTS

- 2 little broccoli crowns (around 8 ounces each)
- 3 tablespoons olive oil
- 1/2 teaspoon salt
- 1/2 teaspoon pepper
- 1/4 teaspoon squashed red pepper chips
- 4 garlic cloves, daintily cut
- 2 tablespoons ground Parmesan cheddar
- 1 teaspoon ground lemon zing

DIRECTIONS

1. Preheat oven to 425°. Cut broccoli crowns into quarters through and through. Shower with oil; sprinkle with salt, pepper and pepper drops. Spot in a material lined 15x10x1-in. skillet.

2. Broil until fresh delicate, 10-12 minutes. Sprinkle with garlic; cook 5 minutes longer. Sprinkle with cheddar; broil until cheddar is dissolved and stalks of broccoli are delicate, 2-4 minutes more. Sprinkle with lemon zing.

61. Keto Spicy Pork Brussels Bowls

PREP TIME: 5 mins COOK TIME: 25 mins TOTAL TIME: 30 mins YIELD: 4 SERVINGS COURSE: Dinner, Lunch, Meal Prep

INGREDIENTS

- olive oil spray
- 1 pound 90% lean ground pork, or swap it for a meatless ground meat option
- 2 tablespoons red wine vinegar
- 3 cloves garlic, minced
- 1 teaspoon smoky paprika
- 2 teaspoons ancho chili powder
- 1 teaspoon kosher salt
- 1/4 teaspoon cayenne pepper
- 1/4 teaspoon freshly ground black pepper
- 1/4 teaspoon dried oregano

- 1/4 teaspoon ground cumin
- 6 cups shredded Brussels sprouts
- 1/4 cup chopped onion
- 4 large eggs

DIRECTIONS:

1. Heat a large cast iron or heavy nonstick skillet over medium heat, spray with oil and cook the meat, breaking it up in small pieces.
2. Combine spices in a small bowl.
3. spices
4. Add garlic, season with spices and vinegar and cook until browned and no longer pink in the middle, 8 to 10 minutes.
5. ground pork in a skillet
6. Set it aside on a plate.
7. Add the Brussels and onions to the pan and cook over high heat, stirring occasionally until the Brussels start to brown and are tender crisp, 6 to 7 minutes.
8. Return the pork to the skillet and mix everything together 1 to 2 minutes.
9. Heat a nonstick skillet or pan and spray with oil, when hot cook the eggs, covered until the

whites are just set and the yolks are still runny, 2 to 3 minutes.

62. Keto Creamy Cauliflower Vegetable Soup

Cooking Time: 20 mins |Total Time: 25 mins |
Servings: 32 bites | Calories: 337kcal

INGREDIENTS:

- 1 pound of cauliflower
- 1 cup of heavy cream
- 2 teaspoons of Salt
- 1 teaspoon pepper white, ground
- 1/2 teaspoon ground nutmeg
- 2 oz. butter salted

DIRECTIONS:

1. Cut the cauliflower into even sized pieces and put them in a pan

2. Add the whipped cream to the pan and fill the pan with water until only the tips of the cauliflower are above the water.

3. Bring the cauliflower to a boil and simmer for 10 minutes, until very tender and break apart easily with a spoon.

4. Add salt, pepper, nutmeg and butter.

5. Mix the soup with a hand blender, being careful not to splash yourself with the hot liquid. We recommend mixing in short bursts until the mixture is smooth.

6. Spoon the soup into 4 bowls to serve and enjoy.

63. Keto Poached Egg Recipe On Smoked Haddock And A Bed Of Spinach

Prep time: 10 minutes |Cooking time: 20 minutes | Yield: 2 servings

INGREDIENTS:

- 2 tablespoons (30 ml) of olive oil for cooking
- 1 shallot, peeled and sliced
- 4 oz. (115 g) baby spinach, stalks
- Salt and pepper , to taste
- 2 fillets of smoked haddock (4 oz. / 115 g each), diced (or use smoked salmon)
- 2 large eggs
- Chives cut to garnish

- 1/3 cup (78 ml) Keto Hollandaise sauce (half the recipe there)

DIRECTIONS:

1. Heat the olive oil in a large saucepan over medium heat and add the shallots. After 30 seconds, add the spinach and stir continuously with a wooden spoon. Cook until the spinach has completely shrunk. Season with salt and pepper and set aside to keep warm.

2. At the same time, bring a pan of water to a boil and add the diced haddock, poaching lightly for 8-10 minutes. Drain and set aside to keep warm.

3. To poach the eggs, bring a pot of water to a boil and then simmer. Crack the eggs one at a time in the water and poach them for 4 minutes, then remove with a slotted spoon and set aside on a paper-lined dish. (Simmer the pan with water as you will need it to make the Hollandaise.)

4. For the Hollandaise sauce, beat the 3 egg yolks with the lemon juice in a bowl that you can easily hold over the pan of boiling water. Continue to beat the mixture while holding the bowl over the heat of the boiling water, keeping a close eye on the heat to prevent the eggs from scrambling. Once light and fluffy, add the melted ghee to the eggs 1 tablespoon at a time, whisking continuously until the ghee is completely absorbed and the Hollandaise has thickened.

5. Before serving, divide the warm spinach between two plates and add the diced haddock. Cover with the poached egg and serve with the hollandaise sauce scooped over.

64. Easy Keto Beef Broccoli

Prep Time: 10 minutes | Cook Time: 25 minutes | Total Time: 35 minutes | Servings: Servings | Calories: 294kcal

INGREDIENTS

- 1 pound flank steak sliced into 1/4 inch thick strips
- 5 cups small broccoli florets about 7 ounces
- 1 tablespoon avocado oil
- For the sauce:
- 1 yellow onion sliced
- 1 Tbs. butter
- ½ tbs. olive oil
- 1/3 cup low-sodium soy sauce
- ⅓ cup beef stock
- 1 tablespoon fresh ginger minced

- 2 cloves garlic minced

DIRECTIONS:

1. Firstly heat avocado oil in a pan over medium heat for a few minutes or until hot.
2. Then add sliced beef and cook until it browns, less than 5 minutes, don't stir too much, you want it to brown. Transfer to a plate and set aside.
3. Add onions to a skillet with butter and olive oil and cook 20 minutes until onions are caramelized and tender.
4. Add all other sauce INGREDIENTS into the pan and stir the INGREDIENTS together over medium-low heat until it starts to simmer, about 5 minutes.
5. Use an absorption blender to blend sauce.
6. Keep the sauce warm over low heat, and add broccoli to the skillet.
7. Then return beef to the pan and toss with broccoli and sauce top. Stir until everything is coated with the sauce.
8. Bring to a simmer and cook for another few minutes until broccoli is tender.

9. Garnish with salt and pepper to taste, if needed.
10. Serve immediately, optionally pairing with cooked cauliflower rice.

65. Asparagus With Hollandaise Sauce

Prep Time: 10 minutes | Cook Time: 5 minutes | Total Time: 15 minutes | Servings: 4 | Calories: 248kcal

INGREDIENTS

- 1 pound asparagus, trimmed
- 1 tablespoon water
- salt and pepper to taste
- Hollandaise Sauce
- 4 ounces salted butter
- 2 large egg yolks
- 1/2 teaspoon Dijon mustard
- 1 tablespoon water
- 1-2 teaspoons freshly squeezed lemon juice (or white vinegar)
- 1-2 pinch cayenne pepper

- 1-2 pinch white pepper

DIRECTIONS:

1. If the asparagus is medium to large in wideness, cut 1 inch off of the bottoms and lightly peel the stalks with a vegetable peeler. I start about 1/3 from the top and continue to the bottom of each spear. If the asparagus is thin, hold a spike towards the bottom and bend it until it snaps. Cut the remaining spears to the same length. Discrete the eggs, reserving the whites for another use.

2. Asparagus:

3. Put the asparagus in a microwave safe bowl and add 1 tablespoon of water. Cover with plastic wrap and cook at high power from 1 1/2 - 2 1/2 minutes depending on your microwave. Drain off the water and keep covered. Alternately, blanch the asparagus in boiling water until it is crunchy tender, drain, and keep warm.

4. Blender Hollandaise

5. Add the egg yolks, 1 tablespoon of water, 1 teaspoon of lemon juice and the mustard to a

blender. Place the lid on top and remove the middle piece. Place the butter in a medium to large frying pan and melt the butter over medium heat. Turn the heat up to medium high and slightly swirl the pan every few moments. When the solids in the bottom of the pan just begin to turn brown, turn off the heat. Turn the blender on low and begin pouring the hot butter into the blender, leaving the brown solids behind in the pan.

6. After the butter has been incorporated, add the cayenne pepper and white pepper and blend. Taste. Adjust seasoning with more acid, salt or pepper. Pour over the asparagus and serve immediately. Serves 4.

66. Keto Keema Curry

Yield: Serves 4 Prep Time: 10 Minutes Cook Time: 40 Minutes Total Time: 50 Minutes

INGREDIENTS

- 450g (1lb) of extra lean beef mince
- 1 large onion, chopped finely
- 1 large carrot, finely chopped
- 1 stalk of celery, finely chopped
- 3 cloves of garlic, crushed
- 1 heaped teaspoon of fresh grated ginger
- 2 teaspoons of cumin seeds
- 2 teaspoon of ground coriander
- 1 teaspoon of deggi mirch Chilli Powder (can add more if you like it really spicy).
- 1 teaspoon of garam masala
- 1 teaspoon of turmeric

- 1 cup of frozen peas
- 4 tablespoons of tomato paste
- cups (600ml) of beef stock (use just 1.5 cups for instant pot)
- freshly chopped coriander to serve
- salt and black pepper
- cooking oil spray (I used avocado)

DIRECTIONS:

1. Stove Top:
2. Spray a frying pan over a medium heat with some spray oil
3. Add the onion, garlic, carrot, celery and ginger and cook for approx. 5 mins to soften.
4. Add the minced beef and cook until browned, breaking up large pieces with the back of a wooden ladle while it cooks.
5. Stir in all the spices (plus the green chili's if using) and tomato paste and mix to evenly coat.
6. Add the stock and bring to a boil, then reduce heat to a simmer until meat is cooked through and stock has reduced to a thicker consistency – approx. 30mins

7. Stir in the peas at the last few minutes.
8. Taste and season as needed with salt and black pepper.
9. Serve topped with freshly chopped coriander and steamed rice.
10. Instant Pot:
11. Set instant pot to sauté mode
12. Add ground beef, onion, celery, carrot, garlic and ginger
13. Fry till beef is browned.
14. Add all other INGREDIENTS (expect peas and coriander)
15. Switch to 12 minutes (high) and ensure valve is closed.
16. When it honks to signal it has done cooking, open the valve to quickly release the pressure.
17. Switch to sauté mode again and simmer for about 1-2 mins just to heat through the peas.
18. Taste and season as needed with salt and black pepper.
19. Serve with chopped fresh coriander and your choice of sides.

67. Keto Stuffed Pepper Recipe

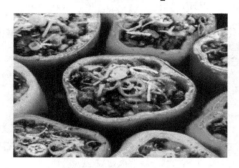

*Preparation Time: 15 mins |Cooking Time: 30 mins |
Total Time: 45 mins| Servings: 6 | Calories: 388kcal*

INGREDIENTS:

- 1 tablespoon of olive oil
- 1 small onion cut into cubes
- Crushed 2 cloves of garlic
- 1 pound ground beef
- 2 tablespoons of Cajun seasoning
- 1 teaspoon of salt
- 1/2 teaspoon ground pepper
- 1/2 cup of tomato passata
- 1 cup of cauliflower rice
- 6 medium peppers
- 1 cup of cheddar cheese shredded
- Common in the US - metric

DIRECTIONS:

1. Preheat your oven to 200C / 390F. Place a large saucepan over high heat and add the oil, onion and garlic. Sauté until the onion starts to turn translucent.

2. Add the ground beef and fry until brown, and then add the Cajun seasoning, salt, pepper, and tomato passata. Mix well.

3. Reduce the heat and let the mixture simmer for 5 minutes.

4. Remove from heat, stir in cauliflower rice and set aside.

5. Prepare the peppers by cutting off the top and removing the seeds and white pith from the inside. Place them in a baking dish with the cut sides facing up.

6. Spoon the ground beef mixture evenly between the peppers and top with cheddar cheese.

7. Bake in the oven for 15-20 minutes until the cheese is brown and the peppers are soft.

8. Serve immediately.

68. Beef liver with bacon recipe

Preparation Time: 10 mins |Cooking Time: 30 mins | Total Time: 40 mins| Servings: 4 | Calories: 297kcal

INGREDIENTS:

- 1-pound grass-fed beef liver
- 4 strips of bacon we use Garrett Valley Uncured Bacon
- Use 3 tablespoons of meadow butter, divided
- ½ large onion
- 4 large cloves of garlic
- 10 grams of sliced mushrooms

DIRECTIONS:

1. Remove the beef liver from the packaging and lay it flat on a paper towel. Pat dry.

2. Generously salt and pepper the liver and let it sit at room temperature while you prepare the remaining INGREDIENTS

3. Dice the bacon and fry in 2 tablespoons butter in a large skillet. When they are crispy, remove the bacon from the pan and drain on kitchen paper. Leave the fat and butter in the pan.

4. Chop the onion coarsely. You want your onion pieces to be about the same size as a piece of liver. The one-to-one ratio is part of the taste secret! Fry on low in bacon fat and butter until it starts to soften but is not yet translucent.

5. Simple beef liver recipe

6. Add garlic to the onions for another 30 seconds.

7. Add mushrooms to the onions and garlic. Fry everything until the mushrooms are cooked.

8. Simple delivery receiver

9. Move all vegetables to one side of the pan, away from the heat. You may want to screw the pan on so that that side is slightly away from the burner.

10. Reduce heat to medium and add the last tablespoon of butter.

11. When the butter has melted, add half of the liver slices. Cook until you start to see the edges cook. They change from red to gray. When that rim is a few millimeters thick (2-3 minutes, or so), flip them over.

12. Fry for another 2-3 minutes on the other side. Until you know how you like your liver, the best way to check it is by cutting it. If it is still red, keep turning until it is barely cooked. You just want a hint of pink so it's cooked through yet soft.

13. Place the liver on a platter and cook the remaining liver in the same way.

14. Toss the bacon cubes through the vegetables and spread the liver with it.

69. Keto Burrito Peppers

Active Time: 15 mins | Total Time: 1 hour | Yield:
Serves: 4 (portion size: 1 stuffed bell pepper)

INGREDIENTS:

- 1 pound ground beef
- ½ cup diced red onion
- 1 teaspoon chili powder
- ¾ teaspoon of kosher salt
- ½ teaspoon of cumin powder
- 2 cups of cauliflower rice
- 1 (5-oz.) Can diced green chilies
- 4 ounces Cheddar cheese, grated (about 1 cup), divided
- 4 tablespoons chopped fresh cilantro, divided
- 4 large bell peppers (any color) or poblano chilies, tops, seeds, and membranes removed

- 4 tablespoons of prepared salsa with no added sugar, divided
- 1 avocado, sliced
- Lime wedges

DIRECTIONS:

1. Preheat the oven to 350 ° F. Heat a large skillet over medium heat. Add ground beef; cook, stirring often to crumble, until browned, about 6 minutes. Add onion and cook, stirring often, until onion softens, about 3 minutes. Add chili powder, salt and cumin; cook, stirring often, until fragrant, about 1 minute.

2. Add cauliflower and cook until tender, about 4 minutes. Stir in green chilies and remove from heat. Stir in 3/4 cup of cheese and 3 tablespoons of cilantro.

3. Generously fill each bell pepper with beef mixture and cover each with 1 tablespoon of salsa. Place the peppers in a 20-inch baking dish and cover with aluminum foil. Bake for 40 minutes in the preheated oven. Remove foil and cover evenly with the remaining cheese. Bake for about 10 minutes until golden and fizzy. Finish with slices of avocado. Sprinkle with the remaining cilantro and serve with lime wedges.

70. Keto Breakfast Burritos

PREPARATION: 20 minutes COOKING TIME: 10 min

TOTAL TIME: 30 min YIELD: 6 SERVINGS

INGREDIENTS:

- 6 strips of bacon cut in the middle
- 10 large eggs, beaten
- 4 spring onions, chopped
- 1/2 red bell pepper, diced
- 1/2 teaspoon of salt
- 12 tablespoons of grated cheddar or pepper jack cheese
- 6 8-inch low-carb flour tortillas (I used Ole Xtreme Wellness)
- 6 pieces Reynolds Wrap Heavy-Duty Aluminum Foil , cut 25 x 30 cm each
- hot sauce for serving, optional

DIRECTIONS:

1. Cook both sides of the tortillas on a hot baking tray or over an open flame. Keep it warm in the oven if you eat right away. This helps the tortillas get smoother and also improves the flavor in my opinion.

2. Heat a large non-stick frying pan over medium heat. Add the bacon and cook until cooked through, about 4 to 5 minutes. Transfer with a slotted spoon to drain onto a paper towel-lined plate.

3. Beat the eggs with salt in a large bowl. Stir in the spring onions and bell pepper.

4. Discard the bacon fat and let stand 1 teaspoon and add the eggs, let them rest on the bottom and stir several times to cook through, set aside.

5. On a clean work surface, spread a generous 1/2 cup of the egg mixture over the bottom third of the tortilla. Top each with a slice of bacon and 2 tablespoons of cheese. Roll from the bottom, fold the left and right corners towards the center and continue to roll into a

tight cylinder. Set aside, seam down, and repeat with remaining tortillas and filling.

6. If you want to eat right away, heat a skillet over medium heat. While hot, spray the pan with oil and add the burritos seam side down. Cook, covered, until the bottom of the burritos is golden brown, about 2 minutes on each side. Serve with hot sauce or salsa, if desired.

71. Avocado Crab Boats

Total Time Prep/Total Time: 20 min. Makes 8 servings

INGREDIENTS

- 5 medium ready avocados, stripped and divided
- 1/2 cup mayonnaise
- 2 tablespoons lemon juice
- 2 jars (6 ounces each) bump crabmeat, depleted
- 4 tablespoons chopped new cilantro, separated
- 2 tablespoons minced chives
- 1 Serrano pepper, cultivated and minced
- 1 tablespoon tricks, depleted
- 1/4 teaspoon pepper
- 1 cup shredded pepper jack cheddar
- 1/2 teaspoon paprika

- Lemon wedges

DIRECTIONS

1. Preheat oven. Spot 2 avocado parts in a large bowl; pound delicately with a fork. Add mayonnaise and lemon juice; blend until very much mixed. Mix in crab, 3 tablespoons cilantro, chives, Serrano pepper, tricks and pepper. Spoon into staying avocado parts.

2. Move to a 15x10x1-in. heating container. Sprinkle with cheddar and paprika. Sear 4-5 in. from heat until cheddar is dissolved, 3-5 minutes. Sprinkle with residual cilantro; present with lemon wedges.

72. Keto meat pie

30 minutes preparation 40 minutes cooking time 6 servings

INGREDIENTS

- Meat filling
- ½ (2 oz.) yellow onion, finely chopped
- 1 garlic clove, finely chopped
- 2 tbsp. butter or olive oil
- 1¼ lbs. ground beef or ground turkey
- 2 tbsp. dried oregano or dried basil
- ½ tsp. salt
- ¼ tsp. ground black pepper
- 3 tbsp. tomato paste
- ½ cup water
- Pie crust
- ¾ cup (3 oz.) almond flour
- ¼ cup (1¼ oz.) sesame seeds

- ¼ cup (¾ oz.) coconut flour
- 1 tbsp. ground psyllium husk powder
- 1 tsp. baking powder
- 1 pinch salt
- 3 tbsp. olive oil
- 1 large egg
- ¼ cup water
- Topping
- 1 cup (7½ oz.) cottage cheese
- 1 cup (4 oz.) cheddar cheese, shredded

DIRECTIONS:

1. Meat filling
2. Firstly preheat the oven to 350°F (175°C).
3. Heat the butter or olive oil in a big frying pan, over medium heat. Add the onion and cook for a few minutes until tender. Add the garlic, ground beef, oregano or basil, salt, and pepper. Use a spatula to break the meat into smaller pieces, while mixing together. Cook for 8-10 minutes or until no longer pink.
4. Add the tomato paste, water, and stir to mix. Reduce heat to medium-low, and simmer

uncovered for 20 minutes, stirring infrequently. Meanwhile, prepare the pie crust.

5. Pie crust

6. Combine the crust INGREDIENTS together using a food processor, or with a fork.

7. Place a round piece of parchment paper in a well-greased, 9-10" (23-25 cm) spring form pan, or deep-dish pie pan. Using a spatula or well-greased fingers, evenly press the dough onto the base and the sides of the pan. Pierce the base and sides of the crust with a fork, to prevent bubbling.

8. Pre-bake the crust for 10 minutes. Remove from the oven and place the meat mixture in the crust.

9. In a little bowl, mix the cottage cheese and shredded cheese. Spread on top of the pie.

10. Bake on the lower rack for 30-40 minutes, or until golden in color.

73. Keto Long Noodle Soup

Total Time Prep/Total Time: 30 min. Makes 6 servings (2 quarts

INGREDIENTS

- 6 ounces uncooked Asian lo Mein noodles
- 1 pork tenderloin (3/4 pound), cut into meager strips
- 2 tablespoons soy sauce, isolated
- 1/8 teaspoon pepper
- 2 tablespoons canola oil, isolated
- 1-1/2 teaspoons minced new gingerroot
- 1 garlic clove, minced
- 1 container (32 ounces) chicken stock

- 1 celery rib, meagerly cut
- 1 cup new snow peas, divided corner to corner
- 1 cup coleslaw blend
- 2 green onions, cut askew
- New cilantro leaves, discretionary

DIRECTIONS

1. Cook noodles as per bundle DIRECTIONS. Channel and flush with cold water; channel well.
2. Then, throw pork with 1 tablespoon soy sauce and pepper. In a 6-qt. stockpot, heat 1 tablespoon oil over medium-high heat; sauté pork until delicately browned, 2-3 minutes. Eliminate from pot.
3. In same pot, heat remaining oil over medium-high heat; sauté ginger and garlic until fragrant, 20-30 seconds. Mix in stock and remaining soy sauce; heat to the point of boiling. Add celery and snow peas; get back to a bubble. Stew, revealed, until fresh delicate, 2-3 minutes. Mix in pork and coleslaw blend; cook just until cabbage starts to shrink. Add

noodles; eliminate from heat. Top with green onions and, whenever wanted, cilantro.

Conclusion

Finish here this food guide and the collection of recipes prepared for you. These recipes contain less carbs and are palatable. Hope these will help you maintaining a healthy life schedule.

I wish you good luck!

CPSIA information can be obtained
at www.ICGtesting.com
Printed in the USA
BVHW090759120521
607041BV00005B/1190